AF147824

A Child's History
of England

VOLUME 2

CHARLES DICKENS

CAMBRIDGE
UNIVERSITY PRESS

CAMBRIDGE
UNIVERSITY PRESS

University Printing House, Cambridge, CB2 8BS, United Kingdom

Cambridge University Press is part of the University of Cambridge.
It furthers the University's mission by disseminating knowledge in the pursuit of
education, learning and research at the highest international levels of excellence.

www.cambridge.org
Information on this title: www.cambridge.org/9781108076784

© in this compilation Cambridge University Press 2015

This edition first published 1853
This digitally printed version 2015

ISBN 978-1-108-07678-4 Paperback

This book reproduces the text of the original edition. The content and language reflect
the beliefs, practices and terminology of their time, and have not been updated.

Cambridge University Press wishes to make clear that the book, unless originally published
by Cambridge, is not being republished by, in association or collaboration with,
or with the endorsement or approval of, the original publisher or its successors in title.

CAMBRIDGE LIBRARY COLLECTION

Books of enduring scholarly value

Education

This series focuses on educational theory and practice, particularly in the context of eighteenth- and nineteenth-century Europe and its colonies, and America. During this period, the questions of who should be educated, to what age, to what standard and using what curriculum, were widely debated. The reform of schools and universities, the drive towards improving women's education, and the movement for free (or at least low-cost) schools for the poor were all major concerns both for governments and for society at large. The books selected for reissue in this series discuss key issues of their time, including the 'appropriate' levels of instruction for the children of the working classes, the emergence of adult education movements, and proposals for the higher education of women. They also cover topics that still resonate today, such as the nature of education, the role of universities in the diffusion of knowledge, and the involvement of religious groups in establishing and running schools.

A Child's History of England

This three-volume history of England from before the Roman conquest through to the Glorious Revolution of 1688 was originally serialised in Charles Dickens' magazine *Household Words* between 1851 and 1853. The text was published in book form in the same period, although each volume was post-dated to the following year. Dickens dedicated the work to his own children, intending it to be a stepping stone to more substantial histories. The volumes were popular with readers for decades, and were used in British schools well into the twentieth century. Dickens employs his signature style to bring events and personalities to life, making use of vivid similes, unabashedly partisan language and direct speech, as well as the occasional moral lesson. Volume 2 covers the period from the reign of Henry III through to the death in 1485 of the 'usurper and murderer' Richard III.

Cambridge University Press has long been a pioneer in the reissuing of out-of-print titles from its own backlist, producing digital reprints of books that are still sought after by scholars and students but could not be reprinted economically using traditional technology. The Cambridge Library Collection extends this activity to a wider range of books which are still of importance to researchers and professionals, either for the source material they contain, or as landmarks in the history of their academic discipline.

Drawing from the world-renowned collections in the Cambridge University Library and other partner libraries, and guided by the advice of experts in each subject area, Cambridge University Press is using state-of-the-art scanning machines in its own Printing House to capture the content of each book selected for inclusion. The files are processed to give a consistently clear, crisp image, and the books finished to the high quality standard for which the Press is recognised around the world. The latest print-on-demand technology ensures that the books will remain available indefinitely, and that orders for single or multiple copies can quickly be supplied.

The Cambridge Library Collection brings back to life books of enduring scholarly value (including out-of-copyright works originally issued by other publishers) across a wide range of disciplines in the humanities and social sciences and in science and technology.

A CHILD'S HISTORY OF ENGLAND.

A

CHILD'S HISTORY OF ENGLAND.

BY

CHARLES DICKENS.

𝔚𝔦𝔱𝔥 𝔞 𝔉𝔯𝔬𝔫𝔱𝔦𝔰𝔭𝔦𝔢𝔠𝔢 𝔟𝔶 𝔍. 𝔚. 𝔗𝔬𝔭𝔥𝔞𝔪.

VOLUME II.

ENGLAND FROM THE REIGN OF HENRY THE THIRD, TO THE
REIGN OF RICHARD THE THIRD.

LONDON:
BRADBURY & EVANS, 11, BOUVERIE STREET.
1853.

TABLE OF THE REIGNS IN VOLUME II.

——◆——

THE PLANTAGENETS—*(Continued.)*

CHRONOLOGICAL TABLE,

AND

TABLE OF CONTENTS TO VOLUME II.

———◆———

CONTENTS.

A CHILD'S HISTORY OF ENGLAND.

CHAPTER XV.

ENGLAND UNDER HENRY THE THIRD, CALLED, OF WINCHESTER.

IF any of the English Barons remembered the murdered Arthur's sister, Eleanor the fair maid of Brittany, shut up in her convent at Bristol, none among them spoke of her now, or maintained her right to the Crown. The dead Usurper's eldest boy, HENRY, by name, was taken by the Earl of Pembroke, the Marshal of England, to the city of Gloucester, and there crowned in great haste when he was only ten years old. As the Crown itself had been lost with the King's treasure, in the raging water, and, as there was no time to make another, they put a circle of plain gold upon his head instead. "We have been the enemies of this child's father," said Lord Pembroke, a good and true gentleman, to the few Lords who were present, "and he merited our ill-will; but the child himself is innocent, and his youth demands our friendship and protection." Those Lords felt tenderly towards the little boy, remembering their own young children ; and they bowed their heads, and said "Long live King Henry the Third!"

Next, a great council met at Bristol, revised Magna Charta, and made Lord Pembroke Regent or Protector of England, as the King was too young to reign alone. The next thing to be done, was, to get rid of Prince Louis of France, and to win over those English Barons who were still ranged under his banner. He was strong in many parts of England, and in London itself; and he held, among other places, a certain Castle called the Castle of Mount Sorel, in Leicestershire. To this fortress, after some skirmishing and truce-making, Lord Pembroke laid siege. Louis despatched an army of six hundred knights and twenty thousand soldiers to relieve it. Lord Pembroke, who was not strong enough for such a force, retired with all his men. The army of the French Prince, which had marched there with fire and plunder, marched away with fire and plunder, and came, in a boastful swaggering manner, to

Lincoln. The town submitted; but the Castle in the town, held by a brave widow lady, named NICHOLA DE CAMVILLE, (whose property it was,) made such a sturdy resistance, that the French Count in command of the army of the French Prince, found it necessary to besiege this Castle. While he was thus engaged, word was brought to him that Lord Pembroke, with four hundred knights, two hundred and fifty men with cross-bows, and a stout force both of horse and foot, was marching towards him. "What care I?" said the French Count. "The Englishman is not so mad as to attack me and my great army in a walled town!" But the Englishman did it for all that, and did it—not so madly but so wisely, that he decoyed the great army into the narrow ill-paved lanes and bye-ways of Lincoln, where its horse-soldiers could not ride in any strong body; and there he made such havoc with them, that the whole force surrendered themselves prisoners, except the Count: who said that he would never yield to any English traitor alive, and accordingly got killed. The end of this victory, which the English called, for a joke, the Fair of Lincoln, was the usual one in those times—the common men were slain without any mercy, and the knights and gentlemen paid ransom and went home.

The wife of Louis, the fair BLANCHE OF CASTILE, dutifully equipped a fleet of eighty good ships, and sent it over from France to her husband's aid. An English fleet of forty ships, some good and some bad, under HUBERT DE BURGH (who had before then been very brave against the French at Dover Castle), gallantly met them near the mouth of the Thames, and took or sunk sixty-five in one fight. This great loss put an end to the French Prince's hopes. A treaty was made at Lambeth, in virtue of which the English Barons who had remained attached to his cause returned to their allegiance, and it was engaged on both sides that the Prince and all his troops should retire peacefully to France. It was time to go; for war had made him so poor that he was obliged to borrow money from the citizens of London to pay his expenses home.

Lord Pembroke afterwards applied himself to governing the country justly, and to healing the quarrels and disturbances that had arisen among men in the days of the bad King John. He caused Magna Charta to be still more improved, and so amended the Forest Laws that a Peasant was no longer put to death for killing a stag in a Royal Forest, but was only imprisoned. It would have been well for England if it could have had so good a Protector many years longer, but that was not to be. Within three years after the young King's Coronation, Lord Pembroke died; and you may see his tomb, at this day, in the old Temple Church in London.

The Protectorship was now divided. PETER DE ROCHES, whom King John had made Bishop of Winchester, was entrusted with the care of the person of the young sovereign; and the exercise of the Royal authority was confided to EARL HUBERT DE BURGH. These two personages had from the first no liking for each other, and soon became enemies. When the young King was declared of age, Peter de Roches, finding that Hubert increased in power and favor, retired discontentedly, and went abroad. For nearly ten years afterwards, Hubert had full sway alone.

But ten years is a long time to hold the favor of a King. This King, too, as he grew up, showed a strong resemblance to his father, in feebleness, inconsistency, and irresolution. The best that can be said of him is that he was not cruel. De Roches coming home again, after ten years, and being a novelty, the King began to favor him and to look coldly on Hubert. Wanting money besides, and having made Hubert rich, he began to dislike Hubert. At last he was made to believe, or pretended to believe, that Hubert had misappropriated some of the Royal treasure; and ordered him to furnish an account of all he had done in his administration. Besides which, the foolish charge was brought against Hubert that he had made himself the King's favorite by magic. Hubert very well knowing that he could never defend himself against such nonsense, and that his old enemy must be determined on his ruin, instead of answering the charges fled to Merton Abbey. Then the King, in a violent passion, sent for the Mayor of London, and said to the Mayor, "Take twenty thousand citizens, and drag me Hubert de Burgh out of that abbey, and bring him here." The Mayor posted off to do it, but the Archbishop of Dublin (who was a friend of Hubert's) warning the King that an abbey was a sacred place, and that if he committed any violence there, he must answer for it to the Church, the King changed his mind and called the Mayor back, and declared that Hubert should have four months to prepare his defence, and should be safe and free during that time.

Hubert, who relied upon the King's word, though I think he was old enough to have known better, came out of Merton Abbey upon these conditions, and journeyed away to see his wife: a Scottish Princess who was then at St. Edmund's Bury.

Almost as soon as he had departed from the Sanctuary, his enemies persuaded the weak King to send out one SIR GODFREY DE CRANCUMB, who commanded three hundred vagabonds called the Black Band, with orders to seize him. They came up with him at a little town in Essex called Brentwood, when he was in bed. He leaped out of bed, got out of the house, fled to the church, ran up to the altar, and laid his hand upon the cross. Sir Godfrey and the Black Band, caring neither for church, altar, nor cross, dragged him forth to the church door, with their drawn swords flashing round his head, and sent for a Smith to rivet a set of chains upon him. When the Smith (I wish I knew his name!) was brought, all dark and swarthy with the smoke of his forge, and panting with the speed he had made; and the Black Band, falling aside to show him the Prisoner, cried with a loud uproar, "Make the fetters heavy! make them strong!" the Smith dropped upon his knee—but not to the Black Band—and said, "This is the brave Earl Hubert de Burgh, who fought at Dover Castle, and destroyed the French fleet, and has done his country much good service. You may kill me, if you like, but I will never make a chain for Earl Hubert de Burgh!"

The Black Band never blushed, or they might have blushed at this. They knocked the Smith about from one to another, and swore at him, and tied the Earl on horseback, undressed as he was, and carried him off to the Tower of London. The Bishops, however, were so indignant at the violation of the Sanctuary of the Church, that the frightened King soon ordered the Black Band to take him back again; at the same time commanding the Sheriff of Essex to prevent his escaping out of Brentwood church. Well! the Sheriff dug a deep trench all round the church, and erected a high fence, and watched the church night and day; the Black Band and their Captain watched it too, like three hundred and one black wolves. For thirty-nine days, Hubert de Burgh remained within. At length, upon the fortieth day, cold and hunger were too much for him, and he gave himself up to the Black Band, who carried him off, for the second time, to the Tower. When his trial came on, he refused to plead; but at last it was arranged that he should give up all the royal lands which had been bestowed upon him, and should be kept at the Castle of Devizes, in what was called "free prison," in charge of four knights appointed by four lords. There, he remained almost a year, until, learning that a follower of his old enemy the Bishop was made Keeper of the Castle, and fearing that he might be killed by treachery, he climbed the ramparts one dark night, dropped from the top of the high Castle wall into the moat, and coming safely to the ground took refuge in another church. From this place he was delivered by a party of horse despatched to his help by some nobles, who were by this time in revolt against the King, and assembled in Wales. He was finally pardoned and restored to his estates, but he lived privately, and never more aspired to a high post in the realm, or to a high place in the King's favor. And thus end—more happily than the stories of many favorites of Kings—the adventures of Earl Hubert de Burgh.

The nobles, who had risen in revolt, were stirred up to rebellion by the overbearing conduct of the Bishop of Winchester, who, finding that the King secretly hated the Great Charter which had been forced from his father, did his utmost to confirm him in that dislike, and in the preference he showed to foreigners over the English. Of this, and of his even publicly declaring that the Barons of England were inferior to those of France, the English Lords complained with such bitterness, that the King, finding them well supported by the clergy, became frightened for his throne, and sent away the Bishop and all his foreign associates.   On his marriage, however, with ELEANOR, a French lady, the daughter of the Count of Provence, he openly favored the foreigners again ; and so many of his wife's relations came over, and made such an immense family-party at court, and got so many good things, and pocketed so much money, and were so high with the English whose money they pocketed, that the bolder English Barons mur-mured openly about a clause there was in the Great Charter, which provided for the banishment of unrea-sonable favorites.   But, the foreigners only laughed disdainfully, and said, " What are your English laws to us ? "

King Philip of France had died, and had been succeeded by Prince Louis, who had also died after a short reign of three years, and had been succeeded by his son of the same name—so moderate and just a man, that he was not the least in the world like a King, as Kings went.   ISABELLA, King Henry's mother, wished very much (for a certain spite she had) that England should make war against this King ; and, as King Henry was a mere puppet in anybody's hands who knew how to manage his feebleness, she easily carried her point with him. But, the Parliament were determined to give him no money for such a war. So, to defy the Parliament, he packed up thirty large casks of silver—I don't know how he got so much; I dare say he screwed it out of the miserable Jews—and put them aboard ship, and went away himself to carry war into France : accompanied by his mother and his brother Richard, Earl of Cornwall, who was rich and clever. But he only got well beaten, and came home.

The good-humour of the Parliament was not restored by this. They reproached the King with wasting the public money to make greedy foreigners rich, and were so stern with him, and so determined not to let him have more of it to waste if they could help it, that he was at his wit's end for some, and tried so shamelessly to get all he could from his subjects, by excuses or by force, that the people used to say the King was the sturdiest beggar in England. He took the Cross, thinking to get some money by that means; but, as it was very well known that he never meant to go on a crusade, he got none. In all this contention, the Londoners were particularly keen against the King, and the King hated them warmly in return. Hating or loving, however, made no difference; he continued in the same condition for nine or ten years, when at last

the Barons said that if he would solemnly confirm
their liberties afresh, the Parliament would vote him a
large sum.

As he readily consented, there was a great meeting
held in Westminster Hall, one pleasant day in May,
when all the clergy, dressed in their robes and holding
every one of them a burning candle in his hand, stood
up (the Barons being also there) while the Archbishop
of Canterbury read the sentence of excommunication
against any man, and all men, who should henceforth,
in any way, infringe the Great Charter of the Kingdom.
When he had done, they all put out their burning
candles with a curse upon the soul of any one, and every
one, who should merit that sentence.   The King concluded with an oath to keep the Charter, "as I am a man,
as I am a Christian, as I am a Knight, as I am a King!"

It was easy to make oaths, and easy to break them;
and the King did both, as his father had done before
him.   He took to his old courses again when he was
supplied with money, and soon cured of their weakness
the few who had ever really trusted him.   When his
money was gone, and he was once more borrowing and
begging everywhere with a meanness worthy of his
nature, he got into a difficulty with the Pope respecting
the Crown of Sicily, which the Pope said he had a

right to give away, and which he offered to King Henry
for his second son, PRINCE EDMUND. But, if you or I
give away what we have not got, and what belongs to
somebody else, it is likely that the person to whom we
give it will have some trouble in taking it. It was
exactly so in this case. It was necessary to conquer
the Sicilian Crown before it could be put upon young
Edmund's head. It could not be conquered without
money. The Pope ordered the clergy to raise money.
The clergy, however, were not so obedient to him as
usual; they had been disputing with him for some
time about his unjust preference of Italian Priests in
England; and they had begun to doubt whether the
King's chaplain, whom he allowed to be paid for
preaching in seven hundred churches, could possibly
be, even by the Pope's favor, in seven hundred places
at once. "The Pope and the King together," said
the Bishop of London, "may take the mitre off my
head; but, if they do, they will find that I shall put
on a soldier's helmet. I pay nothing." The Bishop of
Worcester was as bold as the Bishop of London, and
would pay nothing either. Such sums as the more
timid or more helpless of the clergy did raise were
squandered away, without doing any good to the King,
or bringing the Sicilian Crown an inch nearer to

Prince Edmund's head.   The end of the business was,
that the Pope gave the Crown to the brother of the
King of France (who conquered it for himself), and
sent the King of England in, a bill of one hundred
thousand pounds for the expenses of not having won it·

The King was now so much distressed that we might
almost pity him, if it were possible to pity a King so
shabby and ridiculous.   His clever brother, Richard,
had bought the title of King of the Romans from the
German people, and was no longer near him, to help
him with advice.   The clergy, resisting the very Pope,
were in alliance with the Barons.   The Barons were
headed by SIMON DE MONTFORT, Earl of Leicester,
married to King Henry's sister, and, though a foreigner
himself, the most popular man in England against
the foreign favorites.   When the King next met his
Parliament, the Barons, led by this Earl, came before
him, armed from head to foot, and cased in armour.
When the Parliament again assembled, in a month's
time, at Oxford, this Earl was at their head, and the
King was obliged to consent, on oath, to what was
called a Committee of Government : consisting of
twenty-four members : twelve chosen by the Barons,
and twelve chosen by himself.

But, at a good time for him, his brother Richard

came back. Richard's first act (the Barons would not admit him into England on other terms) was to swear to be faithful to the Committee of Government—which he immediately began to oppose with all his might. Then, the Barons began to quarrel among themselves; especially the proud Earl of Gloucester with the Earl of Leicester, who went abroad in disgust. Then, the people began to be dissatisfied with the Barons, because they did not do enough for them. The King's chances seemed so good again at length, that he took heart enough—or caught it from his brother—to tell the Committee of Government that he abolished them—as to his oath, never mind that, the Pope said!—and to seize all the money in the Mint, and to shut himself up in the Tower of London. Here he was joined by his eldest son, Prince Edward; and, from the Tower, he made public a letter of the Pope's to the world in general, informing all men that he had been an excellent and just King for five-and-forty years.

As everybody knew he had been nothing of the sort, nobody cared much for this document. It so chanced that the proud Earl of Gloucester dying, was succeeded by his son; and that his son, instead of being the enemy of the Earl of Leicester, was (for the time) his friend. It fell out, therefore, that these two Earls joined their forces, took several of the Royal Castles in the country, and advanced as hard as they could on London. The London people, always opposed to the King, declared for them with great joy. The King himself remained shut up, not at all gloriously, in the Tower. Prince Edward made the best of his way to Windsor Castle. His mother, the Queen, attempted to follow him by water; but, the people seeing her barge rowing up the river, and hating her with all their hearts, ran to London Bridge, got together a quantity of stones and mud, and pelted the barge as it came through, crying furiously, "Drown the Witch! Drown her!" They were so near doing it, that the Mayor took the old lady under his protection, and shut her up in St. Paul's until the danger was past.

It would require a great deal of writing on my part, and a great deal of reading on yours, to follow the King through his disputes with the Barons, and to follow the Barons through their disputes with one another—so I will make short work of it for both of us, and only relate the chief events that arose out of these quarrels. The good King of France was asked to decide between them. He gave it as his opinion that the King must maintain the Great Charter, and that the Barons must give up the Committee of Government, and all the rest that had been done by the Parliament at Oxford: which the Royalists, or King's party, scornfully called the Mad Parliament. The Barons declared that these were not fair terms, and they would not accept them. Then, they caused the great bell of St. Paul's to be tolled, for the purpose of rousing up the London people, who armed themselves at the dismal sound and formed· quite an army in the streets. I am sorry to say, however, that instead of falling upon the King's party with whom their quarrel was, they fell upon the miserable Jews, and killed at least five hundred of them. They pretended that some of these Jews were on the King's side, and that they kept hidden in their houses, for the destruction of the people, a certain terrible composition called Greek Fire, which could not be put out with water, but only burnt the fiercer for it. What they really did keep in their houses was money ; and this their cruel enemies wanted, and this their cruel enemies took, like robbers and murderers.

The Earl of Leicester put himself at the head of these Londoners and other forces, and followed the King to Lewes in Sussex, where he lay encamped with his army. Before giving the King's forces battle here, the Earl addressed his soldiers, and said that King Henry the Third had broken so many oaths, that he had become the enemy of God, and therefore they would wear white crosses on their breasts, as if they were arrayed, not against a fellow Christian, but against a Turk.   White-crossed accordingly, they rushed into the fight.   They would have lost the day—the King having on his side all the foreigners in England: and, from Scotland, JOHN COMYN, JOHN BALIOL, and ROBERT BRUCE, with all their men—but for the impatience of PRINCE EDWARD, who, in his hot desire to have vengeance on the people of London, threw the whole of his father's army into confusion. He was taken Prisoner; so was the King; so was the King's brother the King of the Romans; and five thousand Englishmen were left dead upon the bloody grass.

For this success, the Pope excommunicated the Earl of Leicester: which neither the Earl nor the people cared at all about.   The people loved him and supported him, and he became the real King; having all the power of the government in his own hands, though he was outwardly respectful to King Henry the Third, whom he took with him wherever he went, like a poor old limp court-card.   He summoned a Parliament (in the year one thousand two hundred and sixty-five) which was the first Parliament in England that the people had any real share in electing ; and he grew more and more in favor with the people every day, and they stood by him in whatever he did.

Many of the other Barons, and particularly the Earl of Gloucester who had become by this time as proud as his father, grew jealous of this powerful and popular Earl, who was proud too, and began to conspire against him. Since the battle of Lewes, Prince Edward had been kept as a hostage, and, though he was otherwise treated like a Prince, had never been allowed to go out without attendants appointed by the Earl of Leicester, who watched him. The conspiring Lords found means to propose to him, in secret, that they should assist him to escape, and should make him their leader; to which he very heartily consented.

So, on a day that was agreed upon, he said to his attendants after dinner (being then at Hereford), " I should like to ride on horseback, this fine afternoon, a little way into the country." As they, too, thought it would be very pleasant to have a canter in the sunshine, they all rode out of the town together in a gay little troop. When they came to a fine level piece of turf, the Prince fell to comparing their horses one with another, and offering bets that one was faster than another; and the attendants, suspecting no harm, rode galloping

matches until their horses were quite tired. The
Prince rode no matches himself, but looked on from
his saddle, and staked his money. Thus they passed
the whole merry afternoon. Now, the sun was setting,
and they were all going slowly up a hill, the Prince's
horse very fresh and all the other horses very weary,
when a strange rider mounted on a grey steed appeared
at the top of the hill, and waved his hat. "What does
that fellow mean?" said the attendants one to another.
The Prince answered on the instant, by setting spurs
to his horse, dashing away at his utmost speed, joining
the man, riding into the midst of a little crowd of
horsemen who were then seen waiting under some trees,
and who closed around him; and so he departed in a
cloud of dust, leaving the road empty of all but the
baffled attendants, who sat looking at one another, while
their horses drooped their ears and panted.

The Prince joined the Earl of Gloucester at Ludlow.
The Earl of Leicester, with a part of the army and the
stupid old King, was at Hereford. One of the Earl of
Leicester's sons, Simon de Montfort, with another part
of the army was in Sussex. To prevent these two parts
from uniting was the Prince's first object. He attacked
Simon de Montfort by night, defeated him, seized his
banners and treasure, and forced him into Kenil-

worth Castle in Warwickshire, which belonged to his family.

His father, the Earl of Leicester, in the meanwhile, not knowing what had happened, marched out of Hereford, with his part of the army and the King, to meet him. He came, on a bright morning in August, to Evesham, which is watered by the pleasant river Avon. Looking rather anxiously across the prospect towards Kenilworth, he saw his own banners advancing; and his face brightened with joy. But, it clouded darkly when he presently perceived that the banners were captured, and in the enemy's hands; and he said, "It is over. The Lord have mercy on our souls, for our bodies are Prince Edward's!"

He fought like a true Knight, nevertheless. When his horse was killed under him, he fought on foot. It was a fierce battle, and the dead lay in heaps everywhere. The old King, stuck up in a suit of armour on a big war-horse, which didn't mind him at all, and which carried him into all sorts of places where he didn't want to go, got into everybody's way, and very nearly got knocked on the head by one of his son's men. But he managed to pipe out, "I am Harry of Winchester!" and the Prince, who heard him, seized his bridle, and took him out of peril. The Earl of Leicester still

fought bravely, until his best son Henry was killed, and
the bodies of his best friends choked his path; and
then he fell, still fighting, sword in hand.   They
mangled his body, and sent it as a present to a noble
lady—but a very unpleasant lady, I should think,—who
was the wife of his worst enemy.   They could not
mangle his memory in the minds of the faithful people,
though.   Many years afterwards, they loved him more
than ever, and regarded him as a Saint, and always
spoke of him as " Sir Simon the Righteous."

And even though he was dead, the cause for which
he had fought still lived, and was strong, and forced
itself upon the King even in the hour of victory.
Henry found himself obliged to respect the Great
Charter, however much he hated it, and to make laws
similar to the laws of the Great Earl of Leicester, and
to be moderate and forgiving towards the people at
last—even towards the people of London, who had so
long opposed him.   There were more risings before
all this was done, but they were set at rest by these
means, and Prince Edward did his best in all things to
restore peace.   One Sir Adam de Gourdon was the
last dissatisfied knight in arms; but, the Prince
vanquished him in single combat, in a wood, and nobly
gave him his life, and became his friend, instead of

slaying him. Sir Adam was not ungrateful. He ever afterwards remained devoted to his generous conqueror.

When the troubles of the Kingdom were thus calmed, Prince Edward and his cousin Henry took the Cross, and went away to the Holy Land, with many English Lords and Knights. Four years afterwards the King of the Romans died, and, next year, (one thousand two hundred and seventy-two), his brother the weak King of England died. He was sixty-eight years old then, and had reigned fifty-six years. He was as much of a King in death, as he had ever been in life. He was the mere pale shadow of a King at all times.

CHAPTER XVI.

ENGLAND UNDER EDWARD THE FIRST,
CALLED LONGSHANKS.

IT was now the year of our Lord one thousand two hundred and seventy-two; and Prince Edward, the heir to the throne, being away in the Holy Land, knew nothing of his father's death. The Barons, however, proclaimed him King, immediately after the Royal funeral; and the people very willingly consented, since most men knew too well by this time what the horrors of a contest for the crown were. So King Edward the First, called, in a not very complimentary manner, LONGSHANKS, because of the slenderness of his legs, was peacefully accepted by the English Nation.

His legs had need to be strong, however long and thin they were; for they had to support him through many difficulties on the fiery sands of Asia, where his small force of soldiers fainted, died, deserted, and seemed to melt away. But his prowess made light of it, and he said, "I will go on, if I go on with no other follower than my groom!"

A Prince of this spirit gave the Turks a deal of trouble. He stormed Nazareth, at which place, of all places on earth, I am sorry to relate, he made a frightful slaughter of innocent people; and then he went to Acre, where he got a truce of ten years from the Sultan. He had very nearly lost his life in Acre, through the treachery of a Saracen Noble, called the Emir of Jaffa, who, making the pretence that he had some idea of turning Christian and wanted to know all about that religion, sent a trusty messenger to Edward very often—with a dagger in his sleeve. At last, one Friday in Whitsun week, when it was very hot, and all the sandy prospect lay beneath the blazing sun burnt up like a great overdone biscuit, and Edward was lying on a couch, dressed for coolness in only a loose robe, the messenger, with his chocolate-coloured face and his bright dark eyes and white teeth, came creeping in with a letter, and kneeled down like a tame tiger. But, the moment Edward stretched out his hand to take the letter, the tiger made a spring at his heart. He was quick, but Edward was quick too. He seized the traitor by his chocolate throat, threw him to the ground, and slew him with the very dagger he had drawn. The weapon had struck Edward in the arm, and although the wound itself was slight, it threatened to be mortal, for the blade of the dagger had been smeared with poison. Thanks, however, to a better surgeon than was often to be found in those times, and to some wholesome herbs, and above all, to his faithful wife, ELEANOR, who devotedly nursed him, and is said by some to have sucked the poison from the wound with her own red lips (which I am very willing to believe), Edward soon recovered and was sound again.

As the King his father had sent entreaties to him to return home, he now began the journey. He had got as far as Italy, when he met the messengers who brought him intelligence of the King's death. Hearing that all was so quiet at home, he made no haste to return to his own dominions, but paid a visit to the Pope, and went in state through various Italian Towns, where he was welcomed with acclamations as a mighty champion of the Cross from the Holy Land, and where he received presents of purple mantles and prancing horses, and went along in great triumph. The shouting people little knew that he was the last English monarch who would ever embark in a crusade, or that within twenty years every conquest which the Christians had made in the Holy Land at the cost of so much blood, would be won back by the Turks. But all this came to pass.

There was, and there is, an old town standing in a plain in France, called Chalons. When the King was coming towards this place on his way to England, a wily French Lord, called the Count of Chalons, sent him a polite challenge to come with his knights and hold a fair tournament with the Count and *his* knights, and make a day of it with sword and lance. It was represented to the King that the Count of Chalons was not to be trusted, and that, instead of a holiday fight for mere show and in good humour, he secretly meant a real battle, in which the English should be defeated by superior force.

The King, however, nothing afraid, went to the appointed place on the appointed day with a thousand followers. When the Count came with two thousand and attacked the English in earnest, the English rushed at them with such valour that the Count's men and the Count's horses soon began to be tumbled down all over the field. The Count himself seized the King round the neck, but the King tumbled *him* out of his saddle in return for the compliment, and, jumping from his own horse, and standing over him, beat away at his

iron armour like a blacksmith hammering on his anvil.
Even when the Count owned himself defeated and
offered his sword, the King would not do him the
honor to take it, but made him yield it up to a common
soldier. There had been such fury shown in this fight,
that it was afterwards called the little Battle of
Chalons.

The English were very well disposed to be proud of
their King after these adventures; so, when he landed
at Dover in the year one thousand two hundred and
seventy-four (being then thirty-six years old), and went
on to Westminster where he and his good Queen were
crowned with great magnificence, splendid rejoicings
took place. For the coronation-feast there were provided, among other eatables, four hundred oxen, four
hundred sheep, four hundred and fifty pigs, eighteen
wild boars, three hundred flitches of bacon, and twenty
thousand fowls. The fountains and conduits in the
streets flowed with red and white wine instead of water;
the rich citizens hung silks and cloths of the brightest
colours out of their windows to increase the beauty of
the show, and threw out gold and silver by whole
handfuls to make scrambles for the crowd. In short,
there was such eating and drinking, such music and
capering, such a ringing of bells and tossing up of caps,

such a shouting, and singing, and revelling, as the narrow overhanging streets of old London City had not witnessed for many a long day. All the people were merry—except the poor Jews, who, trembling within their houses, and scarcely daring to peep out, began to foresee that they would have to find the money for this joviality sooner or later.

To dismiss this sad subject of the Jews for the present, I am sorry to add that in this reign they were most unmercifully pillaged. They were hanged in great numbers, on accusations of having clipped the King's coin — which all kinds of people had done. They were heavily taxed; they were disgracefully badged; they were, on one day, thirteen years after the coronation, taken up with their wives and children and thrown into beastly prisons, until they purchased their release by paying to the King twelve thousand pounds. Finally, every kind of property belonging to them was seized by the King, except so little as would defray the charge of their taking themselves away into foreign countries. Many years elapsed before the hope of gain induced any of their race to return to England, where they had been treated so heartlessly and had suffered so much.

If King Edward the First had been as bad a king to

Christians as he was to Jews, he would have been bad indeed. But he was, in general, a wise and great monarch, under whom the country much improved. He had no love for the Great Charter—few kings had, through many many years—but he had high qualities. The first bold object that he conceived when he came home, was, to unite under one Sovereign England, Scotland, and Wales; the two last of which countries had each a little king of its own, about whom the people were always quarrelling and fighting, and making a pro- digious disturbance—a great deal more than he was worth. In the course of King Edward's reign he was engaged, besides, in a war with France. To make these quarrels clearer, we will separate their histories and take them thus. Wales, first. France, second. Scotland, third.

LLEWELLYN was the Prince of Wales. He had been on the side of the Barons in the reign of the stupid old King, but had afterwards sworn allegiance to him. When King Edward came to the throne, Llewellyn was required to swear allegiance to him also; which he refused to do. The King, being crowned and in his own dominions, three times more required Llewellyn to come and do homage; and three times more Llewellyn said he would rather not. He was going to be married to ELEANOR DE MONTFORT, a young lady of the family mentioned in the last reign; and it chanced that this young lady, coming from France with her youngest brother, EMERIC, was taken by an English ship, and was ordered by the English King to be detained. Upon this, the quarrel came to a head. The King went, with his fleet, to the coast of Wales, where, so encompassing Llewellyn, that he could only take refuge in the bleak mountain region of Snowdon in which no provisions could reach him, he was soon starved into an apology, and into a treaty of peace, and into paying the expenses of the war. The King, however, forgave him some of the hardest conditions of the treaty, and consented to his marriage. And he now thought he had reduced Wales to obedience.

But, the Welsh, although they were naturally a gentle, quiet, pleasant people, who liked to receive strangers in their cottages among the mountains, and to set before them with free hospitality whatever they had to eat and drink, and to play to them on their harps, and sing their native ballads to them, were a people of great spirit when their blood was up. Englishmen, after this affair, began to be insolent in Wales, and to assume the air of masters; and the Welsh pride

could not bear it. Moreover, they believed in that
unlucky old Merlin, some of whose unlucky old pro-
phecies somebody always seemed doomed to remember
when there was a chance of its doing harm; and just
at this time some blind old gentleman with a harp and
a long white beard, who was an excellent person, but
had become of an unknown age and tedious, burst out
with a declaration that Merlin had predicted that when
English money should become round, a Prince of
Wales would be crowned in London.   Now, King
Edward had recently forbidden the English penny to
be cut up into halves and quarters for halfpence and
farthings, and had actually introduced a round coin;
therefore, the Welsh people said this was the time
Merlin meant, and rose accordingly.

King Edward had bought over PRINCE DAVID,
Llewellyn's brother, by heaping favors upon him;
but he was the first to revolt, being perhaps troubled
in his conscience.   One stormy night, he surprised
the Castle of Hawarden, in possession of which
an English nobleman had been left; killed the whole
garrison, and carried off the nobleman a prisoner to
Snowdon.   Upon this, the Welsh people rose like one
man.   King Edward, with his army, marching from
Worcester to the Menai Strait, crossed it—near to where

the wonderful tubular iron bridge now, in days so different, makes a passage for railway trains—by a bridge of boats that enabled forty men to march abreast. He subdued the Island of Anglesea, and sent his men forward to observe the enemy. The sudden appearance of the Welsh created a panic among them, and they fell back to the bridge. The tide had in the meantime risen and separated the boats; the Welsh pursuing them, they were driven into the sea, and there they sunk, in their heavy iron armour, by thousands. After this victory Llewellyn, helped by the severe winter-weather of Wales, gained another battle; but, the King ordering a portion of his English army to advance through South Wales and catch him between two foes, and Llewellyn bravely turning to meet this new enemy, he was surprised and killed—very meanly, for he was unarmed and defenceless. His head was struck off and sent to London, where it was fixed upon the Tower, encircled with a wreath, some say of ivy, some say of willow, some say of silver, to make it look like a ghastly coin in ridicule of the prediction.

David, however, still held out for six months, though eagerly sought after by the King, and hunted by his own countrymen. One of them finally betrayed him with his wife and children. He was sentenced to be hanged, drawn, and quartered; and, from that time this became the established punishment of Traitors in England—a punishment wholly without excuse, as being revolting, vile, and cruel, after its object is dead; and which has no sense in it, as its only real degradation (and that nothing can blot out), is to the country that permits on any consideration such abominable barbarity.

Wales was now subdued. The Queen giving birth to a young prince in the Castle of Carnarvon, the King showed him to the Welsh people as their countryman, and called him Prince of Wales; a title that has ever since been borne by the heir-apparent to the English Throne—which that little Prince soon became, by the death of his elder brother. The King did better things for the Welsh than that, by improving their laws and encouraging their trade. Disturbances still took place, chiefly occasioned by the avarice and pride of the English Lords, on whom Welsh lands and castles had been bestowed; but they were subdued, and the country never rose again. There is a legend that to prevent the people from being incited to rebellion by the songs of their bards and harpers, Edward had them all put to death. Some of them may have fallen among other men who held out against the King; but this general slaughter is, I think, a fancy of the harpers themselves, who, I dare say, made a song about it many years afterwards, and sang it by the Welsh firesides until it came to be believed.

The foreign war of the reign of Edward the First arose in this way. The crews of two vessels, one a Norman ship, and the other an English ship, happened to go to the same place in their boats to fill their casks with fresh water. Being rough angry fellows, they began to quarrel, and then to fight—the English with their fists; the Normans with their knives—and, in the fight, a Norman was killed. The Norman crew, instead of revenging themselves upon those English sailors with whom they had quarrelled (who were too strong for them, I suspect), took to their ship again in a great rage, attacked the first English ship they met, laid hold of an unoffending merchant who happened to be on board, and brutally hanged him in the rigging of their own vessel with a dog at his feet. This so enraged the English sailors that there was no restraining them; and whenever, and wherever, English sailors met Norman sailors, they fell upon each other tooth and nail. The Irish and Dutch sailors took part with the English; the French and Genoese sailors

D 2

helped the Normans; and thus the greater part of the mariners sailing over the sea became, in their way, as violent and raging as the sea itself when it is disturbed.

King Edward's fame had been so high abroad that he had been chosen to decide a difference between France and another foreign power, and had lived upon the continent three years. At first, neither he nor the French King PHILIP (the good Louis had been dead some time) interfered in these quarrels; but when a fleet of eighty English ships engaged and utterly defeated a Norman fleet of two hundred, in a pitched battle fought round a ship at anchor, in which no quarter was given, the matter became too serious to be passed over. King Edward, as Duke of Guienne, was summoned to present himself before the King of France, at Paris, and answer for the damage done by his sailor subjects. At first, he sent the Bishop of London as his representative, and then his brother EDMUND, who was married to the French Queen's mother. I am afraid Edmund was an easy man, and allowed himself to be talked over by his charming relations, the French court ladies; at all events, he was induced to give up his brother's dukedom for forty days—as a mere form, the French King said, to satisfy

his honour—and he was so very much astonished, when
the time was out, to find that the French King had no
idea of giving it up again, that I should not wonder if
it hastened his death : which soon took place.

King Edward was a King to win his foreign dukedom
back again, if it could be won by energy and valour.
He raised a large army, renounced his allegiance as
Duke of Guienne, and crossed the sea to carry war into
France.   Before any important battle was fought,
however, a truce was agreed upon for two years ; and,
in the course of that time, the Pope effected a reconciliation.   King Edward, who was now a widower,
having lost his affectionate and good wife Eleanor,
married the French King's sister MARGARET ; and the
Prince of Wales was contracted to the French King's
daughter ISABELLA.

Out of bad things, good things sometimes arise. Out
of this hanging of the innocent merchant, and the
bloodshed and strife it caused, there came to be
established one of the greatest powers that the English
people now possess.   The preparations for the war
being very expensive, and King Edward greatly wanting
money, and being very arbitrary in his ways of raising
it, some of the Barons began firmly to oppose him.
Two of them, in particular, HUMPHREY BOHUN, Earl

of Hereford, and ROGER BIGOD, Earl of Norfolk, were
so stout against him, that they maintained he had no
right to command them to head his forces in Guienne,
and flatly refused to go there. "By Heaven, Sir Earl,"
said the King to the Earl of Hereford, in a great
passion, "you shall either go or be hanged!" "By
Heaven, Sir King," replied the Earl of Hereford, "I
will neither go nor yet will I be hanged!" and both he
and the other Earl sturdily left the court, attended by
many Lords. The King tried every means of raising
money. He taxed the clergy in spite of all the Pope
said to the contrary; and when they refused to pay,
reduced them to submission, by saying Very well, then
they had no claim upon the government for protection,
and any man might plunder them who would—which
a good many men were very ready to do, and very
readily did, and which the clergy found too losing a
game to be played at long. He seized all the wool
and leather in the hands of the merchants, promising
to pay for it some fine day; and he set a tax upon the
exportation of wool, which was so unpopular among
the traders that it was called "The evil toll." But all
would not do. The Barons, led by those two great
Earls, declared any taxes imposed without the consent
of Parliament, unlawful; and the Parliament refused

to impose taxes, until the King should confirm afresh the two Great Charters, and should solemnly declare in writing, that there was no power in the country to raise money from the people, evermore, but the power of Parliament representing all ranks of the people. The King was very unwilling to diminish his own power by allowing this great privilege in the Parliament; but there was no help for it, and he at last complied. We shall come to another King by-and-bye, who might have saved his head from rolling off, if he had profited by this example.

The people gained other benefits in Parliament from the good sense and wisdom of this King. Many of the laws were much improved; provision was made for the greater safety of travellers, and the apprehension of thieves and murderers; the priests were prevented from holding too much land, and so becoming too powerful; and Justices of the Peace were first appointed (though not at first under that name) in various parts of the country.

And now we come to Scotland, which was the great and lasting trouble of the reign of King Edward the First.

About thirteen years after King Edward's coronation,

Alexander the Third, the King of Scotland, died of a fall from his horse. He had been married to Margaret, King Edward's sister. All their children being dead, the Scottish crown became the right of a young Princess only eight years old, the daughter of ERIC, King of Norway, who had married a daughter of the deceased sovereign. King Edward proposed, that the Maiden of Norway, as this Princess was called, should be engaged to be married to his eldest son; but, unfortunately, as she was coming over to England she fell sick, and landing on one of the Orkney Islands, died there. A great commotion immediately began in Scotland, where as many as thirteen noisy claimants to the vacant throne started up and made a general confusion.

King Edward being much renowned for his sagacity and justice, it seems to have been agreed to refer the dispute to him. He accepted the trust, and went, with an army, to the Border land where England and Scotland joined. There, he called upon the Scottish gentlemen to meet him at the Castle of Norham, on the English side of the river Tweed; and to that Castle they came. But, before he would take any step in the business, he required those Scottish gentlemen, one and all, to do homage to him as their superior Lord;

and when they hesitated, he said, "By holy Edward, whose crown I wear, I will have my rights, or I will die in maintaining them!" The Scottish gentlemen, who had not expected this, were disconcerted, and asked for three weeks to think about it.

At the end of the three weeks, another meeting took place, on a green plain on the Scottish side of the river. Of all the competitors for the Scottish throne, there were only two who had any real claim, in right of their near kindred to the Royal family. These were JOHN BALIOL and ROBERT BRUCE : and the right was, I have no doubt, on the side of John Baliol. At this particular meeting John Baliol was not present, but Robert Bruce was; and on Robert Bruce being formally asked whether he acknowledged the King of England for his superior lord, he answered, plainly and distinctly, Yes, he did. Next day, John Baliol appeared, and said the same. This point settled, some arrangements were made for inquiring into their titles.

The inquiry occupied a pretty long time—more than a year. While it was going on, King Edward took the opportunity of making a journey through Scotland, and calling upon the Scottish people of all degrees to acknowledge themselves his vassals, or be imprisoned until they did. In the meanwhile, Commissioners were

appointed to conduct the inquiry, a Parliament was
held at Berwick about it, the two claimants were heard
at full length, and there was a vast amount of talking.
At last, in the great hall of the Castle of Berwick, the
King gave judgment in favour of John Baliol: who,
consenting to receive his crown by the King of England's
favour and permission, was crowned at Scone, in an
old stone chair which had been used for ages in the
abbey there, at the coronations of Scottish Kings.
Then, King Edward caused the great seal of Scotland,
used since the late King's death, to be broken in four
pieces, and placed in the English Treasury; and considered that he now had Scotland (according to the
common saying) under his thumb.

Scotland had a strong will of its own yet, however.
King Edward, determined that the Scottish King should
not forget he was his vassal, summoned him repeatedly
to come and defend himself and his Judges before the
English Parliament when appeals from the decisions
of Scottish courts of justice were being heard.   At
length, John Baliol, who had no great heart of his own,
had so much heart put into him by the brave spirit of
the Scottish people, who took this as a national insult,
that he refused to come any more.   Thereupon, the
King further required him to help him in his war

abroad (which was then in progress), and to give up, as security for his good behaviour in future, the three strong Scottish Castles of Jedburgh, Roxburgh, and Berwick. Nothing of this being done; on the contrary, the Scottish people concealing their King among their mountains in the Highlands and showing a determination to resist, Edward marched to Berwick with an army of thirty thousand foot, and four thousand horse; took the Castle, and slew its whole garrison, and the inhabitants of the town as well—men, women, and children. LORD WARRENNE, Earl of Surrey, then went on to the Castle of Dunbar, before which a battle was fought, and the whole Scottish army defeated with great slaughter. The victory being complete, the Earl of Surrey was left as guardian of Scotland; the principal offices in that kingdom were given to Englishmen; the more powerful Scottish Nobles were obliged to come and live in England; the Scottish crown and sceptre were brought away; and even the old stone chair was carried off and placed in Westminster Abbey, where you may see it now. Baliol had the Tower of London lent him for a residence, with permission to range about within a circle of twenty miles. Three years afterwards he was allowed to go to Normandy, where he had estates, and where he passed the remaining six years of his life:

far more happily, I dare say, than he had lived for a
long while in angry Scotland.

Now, there was, in the West of Scotland, a gentleman
of small fortune, named WILLIAM WALLACE, the second
son of a Scottish knight.   He was a man of great size
and great strength; he was very brave and daring;
when he spoke to a body of his countrymen, he could
rouse them in a wonderful manner by the power of his
burning words; he loved Scotland dearly, and he hated
England with his utmost might.   The domineering
conduct of the English who now held the places of
trust in Scotland made them as intolerable to the proud
Scottish people, as they had been, under similar circumstances, to the Welsh; and no man in all Scotland
regarded them with so much smothered rage as William
Wallace.   One day, an Englishman in office, little
knowing what he was, affronted *him*.   Wallace instantly
struck him dead, and taking refuge among the rocks
and hills, and there joining with his countryman, SIR
WILLIAM DOUGLAS, who was also in arms against King
Edward, became the most resolute and undaunted
champion of a people struggling for their independence
that ever lived upon the earth.

The English Guardian of the Kingdom fled before
him, and, thus encouraged, the Scottish people revolted

everywhere, and fell upon the English without mercy. The Earl of Surrey, by the King's commands, raised all the power of the border counties, and two English armies poured into Scotland. Only one Chief, in the face of those armies, stood by Wallace, who, with a force of forty thousand men, awaited the invaders at a place on the river Forth, within two miles of Stirling. Across the river there was only one poor wooden bridge, called the bridge of Kildean—so narrow, that but two men could cross it abreast. With his eyes upon this bridge, Wallace posted the greater part of his men among some rising grounds, and waited calmly. When the English army came up on the opposite bank of the river, messengers were sent forward to offer terms. Wallace sent them back with a defiance, in the name of the freedom of Scotland. Some of the officers of the Earl of Surrey in command of the English, with *their* eyes also on the bridge, advised him to be discreet and not hasty. He, however, urged to immediate battle by some other officers, and particularly by CRES-SINGHAM, King Edward's treasurer, and a rash man, gave the word of command to advance. One thousand English crossed the bridge, two abreast; the Scottish troops were as motionless as stone images. Two thousand English crossed; three thousand, four

thousand, five.   Not a feather, all this time, had been
seen to stir among the Scottish bonnets.   Now, they
all fluttered.   " Forward, one party, to the foot of the
Bridge ! " cried Wallace, " and let no more English
cross !   The rest, down with me on the five thousand
who have come over, and cut them all to pieces ! "   It
was done, in the sight of the whole remainder of the
English army, who could give no help.   Cressingham
himself was killed, and the Scotch made whips for their
horses of his skin.

King Edward was abroad at this time, and during
the successes on the Scottish side which followed, and
which enabled bold Wallace to win the whole country
back again, and even to ravage the English borders.
But, after a few winter months, the King returned, and
took the field with more than his usual energy.   One
night, when a kick from his horse as they both lay on
the ground together broke two of his ribs, and a cry
arose that he was killed, he leaped into his saddle,
regardless of the pain he suffered, and rode through
the camp.   Day then appearing, he gave the word (still,
of course, in that bruised and aching state) Forward !
and led his army on to near Falkirk, where the Scottish
forces were seen drawn up on some stony ground,
behind a morass.   Here, he defeated Wallace, and

killed fifteen thousand of his men.   With the shattered
remainder, Wallace drew back to Stirling; but, being
pursued set fire to the town that it might give no help
to the English, and escaped.   The inhabitants of Perth
afterwards set fire to their houses for the same reason,
and the King, unable to find provisions, was forced to
withdraw his army.

Another ROBERT BRUCE, the grandson of him who
had disputed the Scottish crown with Baliol, was now
in arms against the King (that elder Bruce being dead),
and also JOHN COMYN, Baliol's nephew.   These two
young men might agree with Bruce in opposing Edward,
but could agree in nothing else, as they were rivals for
the throne of Scotland.   Probably it was because they
knew this, and knew what troubles must arise even if they
could hope to get the better of the great English King,
that the principal Scottish people applied to the Pope for
his interference.   The Pope, on the principle of losing
nothing for want of trying to get it, very coolly claimed that
Scotland belonged to him; but this was a little too much,
and the Parliament in a friendly manner told him so.

In the spring time of the year one thousand three
hundred and three, the King sent SIR JOHN SEGRAVE
whom he made Governor of Scotland, with twenty
thousand men, to reduce the rebels.   Sir John was not

as careful as he should have been, but encamped at
Rosslyn, near Edinburgh, with his army divided into
three parts.   The Scottish forces saw their advantage ;
fell on each part separately ; defeated each ; and killed
all the prisoners.   Then, came the King himself once
more, as soon as a great army could be raised ; he
passed through the whole north of Scotland, laying
waste whatsoever came in his way ; and he took up his
winter quarters at Dunfermline.   The Scottish cause
now looked so hopeless, that Comyn and the other
nobles made submission and received their pardons.
Wallace alone stood out.   He was invited to surrender,
though on no distinct pledge that his life should be
spared ; but he still defied the ireful King, and lived
among the steep crags of the Highland glens, where the
eagles made their nests, and where the mountain
torrents roared, and the white snow was deep, and the
bitter winds blew round his unsheltered head, as he lay
through many a pitch-dark night wrapped up in his
plaid.   Nothing could break his spirit ; nothing could
lower his courage ; nothing could induce him to forget
or to forgive his country's wrongs.   Even when the
Castle of Stirling, which had long held out, was besieged
by the King with every kind of military engine then in
use ; even when the lead upon cathedral roofs was

taken down to help to make them; even when the King, though now an old man, commanded in the siege as if he were a youth, being so resolved to conquer; even when the brave garrison (then found with amazement to be not two hundred people, including several ladies) were starved and beaten out and were made to submit on their knees, and with every form of disgrace that could aggravate their sufferings; even then, when there was not a ray of hope in Scotland, William Wallace was as proud and firm as if he had beheld the powerful and relentless Edward lying dead at his feet.

Who betrayed William Wallace in the end, is not quite certain. That he was betrayed—probably by an attendant—is too true. He was taken to the Castle of Dumbarton, under SIR JOHN MENTEITH, and thence to London, where the great fame of his bravery and resolution attracted immense concourses of people, to behold him. He was tried in Westminster Hall, with a crown of laurel on his head—it is supposed because he was reported to have said that he ought to wear, or that he would wear, a crown there—and was found guilty as a robber, a murderer, and a traitor. What they called a robber (he said to those who tried him) he was, because he had taken spoil from the King's men. What they called a murderer, he was, because

he had slain an insolent Englishman. What they
called a traitor, he was not, for he had never sworn
allegiance to the King, and had ever scorned to do it.
He was dragged at the tails of horses to West Smithfield, and there hanged on a high gallows, torn open
before he was dead, beheaded, and quartered. His
head was set upon a pole on London Bridge, his right
arm was sent to Newcastle, his left arm to Berwick, his
legs to Perth and Aberdeen. But, if King Edward had
had his body cut into inches, and had sent every separate
inch into a separate town, he could not have dispersed
it half so far and wide as his fame. Wallace will be
remembered in songs and stories, while there are songs
and stories in the English tongue, and Scotland will
hold him dear while her lakes and mountains last.

Released from this dreaded enemy, the King made a
fairer plan of Government for Scotland, divided the
offices of honor among Scottish gentlemen and English
gentlemen, forgave past offences, and thought, in his
old age, that his work was done.

But he deceived himself. Comyn and Bruce con-
spired, and made an appointment to meet at Dum-
fries, in the church of the Minorites. There is a story
that Comyn was false to Bruce, and had informed
against him to the King; that Bruce was warned of his

danger and the necessity of flight, by receiving, one
night as he sat at supper, from his friend the Earl of
Gloucester, twelve pennies and a pair of spurs; that as
he was riding angrily to keep his appointment (through
a snow-storm, with his horse's shoes reversed that he
might not be tracked), he met an evil-looking serving
man, a messenger of Comyn, whom he killed, and concealed in whose dress he found letters that proved
Comyn's treachery. However this may be, they were
likely enough to quarrel in any case, being hot-headed
rivals; and, whatever they quarrelled about, they
certainly did quarrel in the church where they met,
and Bruce drew his dagger and stabbed Comyn, who
fell upon the pavement. When Bruce came out, pale
and disturbed, the friends who were waiting for him,
asked what was the matter? "I think I have killed
Comyn," said he. "You only think so?" returned
one of them; "I will make sure!" and going into the
church, and finding him alive, stabbed him again and
again. Knowing that the King would never forgive this
new deed of violence, the party then declared Bruce
King of Scotland: got him crowned at Scone—without
the chair; and set up the rebellious standard once again.

When the King heard of it he kindled with fiercer
anger than he had ever shown yet. He caused the

E 2

Prince of Wales and two hundred and seventy of the young nobility to be knighted—the trees in the Temple Gardens were cut down to make room for their tents, and they watched their armour all night, according to the old usage: some in the Temple Church: some in Westminster Abbey—and at the public Feast which then took place, he swore, by Heaven, and by two swans covered with gold network which his minstrels placed upon the table, that he would avenge the death of Comyn, and would punish the false Bruce. And before all the company, he charged the Prince his son, in case that he should die before accomplishing this vow, not to bury him until it was fulfilled. Next morning the Prince and the rest of the young Knights rode away to the Border country to join the English army; and the King, now weak and sick, followed in a horse-litter.

Bruce, after losing a battle and undergoing many dangers and much misery, fled to Ireland, where he lay concealed through the winter. That winter, Edward passed in hunting down and executing Bruce's relations and adherents, sparing neither youth nor age, and showing no touch of pity or sign of mercy. In the following spring, Bruce re-appeared and gained some victories. In these frays, both sides were grievously cruel. For instance—Bruce's two brothers, being taken captives desperately wounded, were ordered by the King to instant execution. Bruce's friend Sir John Douglas, taking his own Castle of Douglas out of the hands of an English Lord, roasted the dead bodies of the slaughtered garrison in a great fire made of every moveable within it; which dreadful cookery his men called the Douglas Larder. Bruce, still successful, however, drove the Earl of Pembroke and the Earl of Gloucester into the Castle of Ayr and laid siege to it.

The King, who had been laid up all the winter, but had directed the army from his sick-bed, now advanced to Carlisle, and there, causing the litter in which he had travelled to be placed in the Cathedral as an offering to Heaven, mounted his horse once more, and for the last time. He was now sixty-nine years old, and had reigned thirty-five years. He was so ill, that in four days he could go no more than six miles; still, even at that pace, he went on and resolutely kept his face towards the Border. At length, he lay down at the village of Burgh-upon-Sands; and there, telling those around him to impress upon the Prince that he was to remember his father's vow, and was never to rest until he had thoroughly subdued Scotland, he yielded up his last breath.

CHAPTER XVII.

ENGLAND UNDER EDWARD THE SECOND.

KING Edward the Second, the first Prince of Wales, was twenty-three years old when his father died. There was a certain favorite of his, a young man from Gascony, named PIERS GAVESTON, of whom his father had so much disapproved that he had ordered him out of England, and had made his son swear by the side of his sick-bed, never to bring him back. But, the Prince no sooner found himself King, than he broke his oath, as so many other Princes and Kings did (they were far too ready to take oaths), and sent for his dear friend immediately.

Now, this same Gaveston was handsome enough, but was a reckless, insolent, audacious fellow. He was detested by the proud English Lords : not only because he had such power over the King, and made the Court such a dissipated place, but, also, because he could ride better than they at tournaments, and was used, in his impudence, to cut very bad jokes on them; calling one, the old hog; another, the stage-player; another, the Jew; another, the black dog of Ardenne. This was as poor wit as need be, but it made those Lords very wroth; and the surly Earl of Warwick, who was the black dog, swore that the time should come when Piers Gaveston should feel the black dog's teeth.

It was not come yet, however, nor did it seem to be coming. The King made him Earl of Cornwall, and gave him vast riches; and, when the King went over to France to marry the French Princess, ISABELLA, daughter of PHILIP LE BEL: who was said to be the most beautiful woman in the world: he made Gaveston, Regent of the Kingdom. His splendid marriage-ceremony in the Church of Our Lady at Boulogne, where there were four Kings and three Queens present (quite a pack of Court Cards, for I dare say the Knaves were not wanting), being over, he seemed to care little or nothing for his beautiful wife; but was wild with impatience to meet Gaveston again.

When he landed at home, he paid no attention to anybody else, but ran into the favorite's arms before a great concourse of people, and hugged him, and kissed him, and called him his brother. At the coronation which soon followed, Gaveston was the richest and brightest of all the glittering company there, and had the honor of carrying the crown. This made the proud Lords fiercer than ever; the people, too, despised the favorite, and would never call him Earl of Cornwall, however much he complained to the King and asked him to punish them for not doing so, but persisted in styling him plain Piers Gaveston.

The Barons were so unceremonious with the King in giving him to understand that they would not bear this favorite, that the King was obliged to send him out of the country. The favorite himself was made to take an oath (more oaths!) that he would never come back, and the Barons supposed him to be banished in disgrace, until they heard · that he was appointed Governor of Ireland. Even this was not enough for the besotted King, who brought ·him home again in a year's time, and not only disgusted the Court and the people by his doting folly, but offended his beautiful wife too, who never liked him afterwards.

He had now the old Royal want—of money—and the Barons had the new power of positively refusing to let him raise any. He summoned a Parliament at York; the Barons refused to make one, while the favorite was near him. He summoned another

Parliament at Westminster, and sent Gaveston away. Then, the Barons came, completely armed, and appointed a committee of themselves, to correct abuses in the state and in the King's household. He got some money on these conditions, and directly set off with Gaveston to the Border-country, where they spent it in idling away the time, and feasting, while Bruce made ready to drive the English out of Scotland. For, though the old King had even made this poor weak son of his swear (as some say) that he would not bury his bones, but would have them boiled clean in a caldron, and carried before the English army until Scotland was entirely subdued, the second Edward was so unlike the first that Bruce gained strength and power every day.

The committee of Nobles, after some months of deliberation, ordained that the King should henceforth call a Parliament together, once every year, and even twice if necessary, instead of summoning it only when he chose. Further, that Gaveston should once more be banished, and, this time, on pain of death if he ever came back. The King's tears were of no avail; he was obliged to send his favorite to Flanders. As soon as he had done so, however, he dissolved the Parliament, with the low cunning of a mere fool, and set off to the

North of England, thinking to get an army about him
to oppose the Nobles. And once again he brought
Gaveston home, and heaped upon him all the riches
and titles of which the Barons had deprived him.

The Lords saw, now, that there was nothing for
it but to put the favorite to death. They could
have done so, legally, according to the terms of his
banishment; but they did so, I am sorry to say, in
a shabby manner. Led by the Earl of Lancaster,
the King's cousin, they first of all attacked the King
and Gaveston at Newcastle. They had time to escape
by sea, and the mean King, having his precious
Gaveston with him, was quite content to leave his
lovely wife behind. When they were comparatively
safe, they separated; the King went to York to collect
a force of soldiers; and the favorite shut himself up,
in the meantime, in Scarborough Castle over-looking
the sea. This was what the Barons wanted. They
knew that the Castle could not hold out; they attacked
it, and made Gaveston surrender. He delivered
himself up to the Earl of Pembroke—that Lord whom
he had called the Jew—on the Earl's pledging his faith
and knightly word, that no harm should happen to him
and no violence be done him.

Now, it was agreed with Gaveston that he should be

taken to the Castle of Wallingford, and there kept in honorable custody. They travelled as far as Dedington, near Banbury, where, in the Castle of that place, they stopped for a night to rest. Whether the Earl of Pembroke left his prisoner there, knowing what would happen, or really left him thinking no harm, and only going (as he pretended) to visit his wife, the Countess, who was in the neighbourhood, is no great matter now; in any case, he was bound as an honorable gentleman to protect his prisoner, and he did not do it. In the morning, while the favorite was yet in bed, he was required to dress himself and come down into the court-yard. He did so without any mistrust, but started and turned pale when he found it full of strange armed men. "I think you know me?" said their leader, also armed from head to foot. "I am the black dog of Ardenne!"

The time was come when Piers Gaveston was to feel the black dog's teeth indeed. They set him on a mule, and carried him, in mock state and with military music, to the black dog's kennel—Warwick Castle—where a hasty council, composed of some great noblemen, considered what should be done with him. Some were for sparing him, but one loud voice—it was the black dog's bark, I dare say—sounded through the Castle

Hall, uttering these words : " You have the fox in
your power. Let him go now, and you must hunt
him again."

They sentenced him to death. He threw himself at
the feet of the Earl of Lancaster—the old hog—but
the old hog was as savage as the dog. He was taken
out upon the pleasant road, leading from Warwick to
Coventry, where the beautiful river Avon, by which,
long afterwards, WILLIAM SHAKESPEARE was born and
now lies buried, sparkled in the bright landscape of
the beautiful May-day ; and there they struck off his
wretched head, and stained the dust with his blood.

When the King heard of this black deed, in his
grief and rage he denounced relentless war against his
Barons, and both sides were in arms for half-a-year.
But, it then became necessary for them to join their
forces against Bruce, who had used the time well while
they were divided, and had now a great power in
Scotland.

Intelligence was brought that Bruce was then
besieging Stirling Castle, and that the Governor had
been obliged to pledge himself to surrender it, unless
he should be relieved before a certain day. Hereupon,
the King ordered the nobles and their fighting-men to
meet him at Berwick; but, the nobles cared so little

for the King, and so neglected the summons, and lost time, that only on the day before that appointed for the surrender, did the King find himself at Stirling, and even then with a smaller force than he had expected. However, he had, altogether, a hundred thousand men, and Bruce had not more than forty thousand; but, Bruce's army was strongly posted in three square columns, on the ground lying between the Burn or Brook of Bannock and the walls of Stirling Castle.

On the very evening, when the King came up, Bruce did a brave act that encouraged his men. He was seen by a certain HENRY DE BOHUN, an English Knight, riding about before his army on a little horse, with a light battle-axe in his hand, and a crown of gold on his head. This English Knight, who was mounted on a strong war-horse, cased in steel, strongly armed, and able (as he thought) to overthrow Bruce by crushing him with his mere weight, set spurs to his great charger, rode on him, and made a thrust at him with his heavy spear. Bruce parried the thrust, and with one blow of his battle-axe split his skull.

The Scottish men did not forget this, next day when the battle raged. RANDOLPH, Bruce's valiant Nephew, rode, with the small body of men he commanded, into such a host of the English, all shining in polished armour in the sunlight, that they seemed to be swallowed up and lost, as if they had plunged into the sea.   But, they fought so well, and did such dreadful execution, that the English staggered.   Then came Bruce himself upon them, with all the rest of his army.   While they were thus hard pressed and amazed, there appeared upon the hills what they supposed to be a new Scottish army, but what were really only the camp followers, in number fifteen thousand : whom Bruce had taught to show themselves at that place and time.   The Earl of Gloucester, commanding the English horse, made a last rush to change the fortune of the day; but, Bruce (like Jack the Giant-killer in the story) had had pits dug in the ground, and covered over with turfs and stakes.   Into these, as they gave way beneath the weight of the horses, riders and horses rolled by hundreds.   The English were completely routed; all their treasure, stores, and engines, were taken by the Scottish men; so many waggons and other wheeled vehicles were seized, that it is related that they would have reached, if they had been drawn out in a line, one hundred and eighty miles. The fortunes of Scotland were, for the time, completely changed; and never was a battle won, more famous

upon Scottish ground, than this great battle of
BANNOCKBURN.

Plague and famine succeeded in England; and still
the powerless King and his disdainful Lords were
always in contention. Some of the turbulent chiefs of
Ireland made proposals to Bruce, to accept the rule of
that country. He sent his brother Edward to them,
who was crowned King of Ireland. He afterwards
went himself to help his brother in his Irish wars, but
his brother was defeated in the end and killed. Robert
Bruce, returning to Scotland, still increased his strength
there.

As the King's ruin had begun in a favorite, so it
seemed likely to end in one. He was too poor a creature
to rely at all upon himself; and his new favorite was
one HUGH LE DESPENSER, the son of a gentleman of an
ancient family. Hugh was handsome and brave, but
he was the favorite of a weak King, whom no man
cared a rush for, and that was a dangerous place to
hold. The Nobles leagued against him, because the
King liked him; and they lay in wait, both for his ruin
and his father's. Now, the King had married him to
the daughter of the late Earl of Gloucester, and had
given both him and his father great possessions in
Wales. In their endeavours to extend these, they gave

violent offence to an angry Welsh gentleman, named
JOHN DE MOWBRAY, and to divers other angry Welsh
gentlemen, who resorted to arms, took their castles, and
seized their estates.   The Earl of Lancaster had first
placed the favorite (who was a poor relation of his own)
at Court, and he considered his own dignity offended
by the preference he received and the honors he
acquired ; so he, and the Barons who were his friends,
joined the Welshmen, marched on London, and sent a
message to the King demanding to have the favorite
and his father banished.   At first, the King unaccount-
ably took it into his head to be spirited, and to send
them a bold reply; but when they quartered themselves around Holborn and Clerkenwell, and went down,
armed, to the Parliament at Westminster, he gave way,
and complied with their demands.

His turn of triumph came sooner than he expected.
It arose out of an accidental circumstance.   The beautiful Queen happening to be travelling, came one night
to one of the royal castles, and demanded to be lodged
and entertained there until morning.   The governor
of this castle, who was one of the enraged lords, was
away, and in his absence, his wife refused admission
to the Queen; a scuffle took place among the common
men on either side, and some of the royal attendants

were killed. The people, who cared nothing for the King, were very angry that their beautiful Queen should be thus rudely treated in her own dominions; and the King, taking advantage of this feeling, besieged the castle, took it, and then recalled the two Despensers home. Upon this, the confederate lords and the Welshmen went over to Bruce. The King encountered them at Boroughbridge, gained the victory, and took a number of distinguished prisoners; among them, the Earl of Lancaster, now an old man, upon whose destruction he was resolved. This Earl was taken to his own castle of Pontefract, and there tried and found guilty by an unfair court appointed for the purpose; he was not even allowed to speak in his own defence. He was insulted, pelted, mounted on a starved pony without saddle or bridle, carried out, and beheaded. Eight-and-twenty knights were hanged, drawn, and quartered. When the King had despatched this bloody work, and had made a fresh and a long truce with Bruce, he took the Despensers into greater favor than ever, and made the father Earl of Winchester.

One prisoner, and an important one, who was taken at Boroughbridge, made his escape, however, and turned the tide against the King. This was ROGER MORTIMER, always resolutely opposed to him, who was sentenced to death, and placed for safe-custody in the Tower of London.   He treated his guards to a quantity of wine into which he had put a sleeping potion; and, when they were insensible, broke out of his dungeon, got into a kitchen, climbed up the chimney, let himself down from the roof of the building with a rope-ladder, passed the sentries, got down to the river, and made away in a boat to where servants and horses were waiting for him.   He finally escaped to France, where CHARLES LE BEL, the brother of the beautiful Queen, was King. Charles sought to quarrel with the King of England, on pretence of his not having come to do him homage at his coronation.   It was proposed that the beautiful Queen should go over to arrange the dispute; she went, and wrote home to the King, that as he was sick and could not come to France himself, perhaps it would be better to send over the young Prince, their son, who was only twelve years old, who could do homage to her brother in his stead, and in whose company she would immediately return.   The King sent him: but, both he and the Queen remained at the French court, and Roger Mortimer became the Queen's lover.

When the King wrote, again and again, to the Queen to come home, she did not reply that she despised him too much to live with him any more (which was the truth), but said she was afraid of the two Despensers. In short, her design was to overthrow the favorites' power, and the King's power, such as it was, and invade England. Having obtained a French force of two thousand men, and being joined by all the English exiles then in France, she landed, within a year, at Orewell, in Suffolk, where she was immediately joined by the Earls of Kent and Norfolk, the King's two brothers; by other powerful noblemen; and lastly, by the first English general who was despatched to check her : who went over to her with all his men. The people of London, receiving these tidings, would do nothing for the King, but broke open the Tower, let out all his prisoners, and threw up their caps and hurrahed for the beautiful Queen.

The King, with his two favorites, fled to Bristol, where he left old Despenser in charge of the town and castle, while he went on with the son to Wales. The Bristol men being opposed to the King, and it being impossible to hold the town with enemies everywhere within the walls, Despenser yielded it up on the third day, and was instantly brought to trial for having traitorously influenced what was called " the King's mind "—though I doubt if the King ever had any. He was a venerable old man, upwards of ninety years of age, but his age gained no respect or mercy. He was hanged, torn open while he was yet alive, cut up into pieces, and thrown to the dogs. His son was soon taken, tried at Hereford before the same judge on a long series of foolish charges, found guilty, and hanged. upon a gallows fifty feet high, with a chaplet of nettles round his head. His poor old father and he were innocent enough of any worse crimes than the crime of having been the friends of a King, on whom, as a mere man, they would never have deigned to cast a favorable look. It is a bad crime, I know, and leads to worse; but, many lords and gentlemen—I even think some ladies, too, if I recollect right—have committed it in England, who have neither been given to the dogs, nor hanged up fifty feet high.

The wretched King was running here and there, all this time, and never getting anywhere in particular, until he gave himself up, and was taken off to Kenilworth Castle. When he was safely lodged there, the Queen went to London and met the Parliament. And the Bishop of Hereford, who was the most skilful of her friends, said, What was to be done now? Here was an imbecile, indolent, miserable King upon the throne; wouldn't it be better to take him off, and put his son there instead? I don't know whether the

Queen really pitied him at this pass, but she began to cry; so, the Bishop said, Well, my Lords and Gentlemen, what do you think, upon the whole, of sending down to Kenilworth, and seeing if His Majesty (God bless him, and forbid we should depose him!) won't resign?

My Lords and Gentlemen thought it a good notion, so a deputation of them went down to Kenilworth; and there the King came into the great hall of the Castle, commonly dressed in a poor black gown; and when he saw a certain bishop among them, fell down, poor feeble-headed man, and made a wretched spectacle of himself. Somebody lifted him up, and then SIR WILLIAM TRUSSEL, the Speaker of the House of Commons, almost frightened him to death by making him a tremendous speech, to the effect that he was no longer a King, and that everybody renounced allegiance to him. After which, SIR THOMAS BLOUNT, the Steward of the Household, nearly finished him, by coming forward and breaking his white wand—which was a ceremony only performed at a King's death. Being asked in this pressing manner what he thought of resigning, the King said he thought it was the best thing he could do. So, he did it, and they proclaimed his son next day.

I wish I could close his history by saying that he lived a harmless life in the Castle and the Castle gardens at Kenilworth, many years—that he had a favorite, and plenty to eat and drink—and, having that, wanted nothing. But he was shamefully humiliated. He was outraged, and slighted, and had dirty water from ditches given him to shave with, and wept and said he would have clean warm water, and was altogether very miserable. He was moved from this castle to that castle, and from that castle to the other castle, because this lord or that lord, or the other lord, was too kind to him : until at last he came to Berkeley Castle, near the River Severn, where (the Lord Berkeley being then ill and absent) he fell into the hands of two black ruffians called THOMAS GOURNAY, and WILLIAM OGLE.

One night—it was the night of September the twenty-first, one thousand three hundred and twenty-seven—dreadful screams were heard, by the startled people in the neighbouring town, ringing through the thick walls of the Castle, and the dark deep night ; and they said, as they were thus horribly awakened from their sleep, "May Heaven be merciful to the King ; for those cries forbode that no good is being done to him in his dismal prison !"   Next morning he was dead—not bruised, or stabbed, or marked upon the body, but much distorted in the face ; and it was whispered afterwards, that those two villains, Gournay and Ogle, had burnt up his inside with a red-hot iron.

If you ever come near Gloucester, and see the centre tower of its beautiful Cathedral, with its four rich pinnacles, rising lightly in the air; you may remember that the wretched Edward the Second was buried in the old abbey of that ancient city, at forty-three years old, after being for nineteen years and a half a perfectly incapable King.

CHAPTER XVIII.

ENGLAND UNDER EDWARD THE THIRD.

ROGER MORTIMER, the Queen's lover (who escaped to France in the last chapter), was far from profiting by the examples he had had of the fate of favorites. Having, through the Queen's influence, come into possession of the estates of the two Despensers, he became extremely proud and ambitious, and sought to be the real ruler of England. The young King, who was crowned at fourteen years of age with all the usual solemnities, resolved not to bear this, and soon pursued Mortimer to his ruin.

The people themselves were not fond of Mortimer—first, because he was a Royal favorite; secondly, because he was supposed to have helped to make a peace with Scotland which now took place, and in virtue of which the young King's sister Joan, only seven years old, was promised in marriage to David, the son and heir of Robert Bruce, who was only five years old.   The nobles hated Mortimer because of his pride, riches, and power.   They went so far as to take up arms against him; but were obliged to submit.   The Earl of Kent, one of those who did so, but who after- wards went over to Mortimer and the Queen, was made an example of in the following cruel manner:

He seems to have been anything but a wise old earl; and he was persuaded by the agents of the favorite and the Queen, that poor King Edward the Second was not really dead; and thus was betrayed into writing letters favoring his rightful claim to the throne.   This was made out to be high treason, and he was tried, found guilty, and sentenced to be executed.   They took the poor old lord outside the town of Winchester, and there kept him waiting some three or four hours until they could find somebody to cut off his head.   At last, a convict said he would do it, if the government would pardon him in return; and they gave him the pardon; and at one blow he put the Earl of Kent out of his last suspense.

While the Queen was in France, she had found a lovely and good young lady, named Phillipa, who she thought would make an excellent wife for her son. The young King married this lady, soon after he came to the throne ; and her first child, Edward, Prince of Wales, afterwards became celebrated, as we shall presently see, under the famous title of EDWARD THE BLACK PRINCE.

The young King, thinking the time ripe for the downfall of Mortimer, took counsel with Lord Montacute how he should proceed. A Parliament was going to be held at Nottingham, and that lord recommended that the favorite should be seized by night in Nottingham Castle, where he was sure to be. Now, this, like many other things, was more easily said than done ; because, to guard against treachery, the great gates of the Castle were locked every night, and the great keys were carried up-stairs to the Queen, who laid them under her own pillow. But the Castle had a governor, and, the governor being Lord Montacute's friend, confided to him how he knew of a secret passage underground, hidden from observation by the weeds and brambles with which it was overgrown ; and how, through that passage, the conspirators might enter in the dead of night, and go straight to Mortimer's room. Accordingly, upon a certain dark night, at midnight, they made their way through this dismal place : startling the rats, and frightening the owls and bats : and came safely to the bottom of the main tower of the Castle, where the King met them, and took them up a profoundly-dark staircase in a deep silence. They soon heard the voice of Mortimer in council with some friends; and bursting into the room with a sudden noise, took him prisoner. The Queen cried out from her bed-chamber, " Oh, my sweet son, my dear son, spare my gentle Mortimer!" They carried him off, however; and, before the next Parliament, accused him of having made differences between the young King and his mother, and of having brought about the death of the Earl of Kent, and even of the late King; for, as you know by this time, when they wanted to get rid of a man in those old days, they were not very particular of what they accused him. Mortimer was found guilty of all this, and was sentenced to be hanged at Tyburn. The King shut his mother up in genteel confinement, where she passed the rest of her life; and now he became King in earnest.

The first effort he made was to conquer Scotland. The English lords who had lands in Scotland, finding that their rights were not respected under the late peace, made war on their own account: choosing for their general, Edward, the son of John Baliol, who made such a vigorous fight, that in less than two months he won the whole Scottish Kingdom. He was joined, when thus triumphant, by the King and Parliament; and he and the King in person besieged the Scottish forces in Berwick. The whole Scottish army coming to the assistance of their countrymen, such a furious battle ensued, that thirty thousand men are said to have been killed in it. Baliol was then crowned King of Scotland, doing homage to the King of England; but little came of his successes after all, for the Scottish men rose against him, within no very long time, and David Bruce came back within ten years and took his kingdom.

France was a far richer country than Scotland, and the King had a much greater mind to conquer it. So, he let Scotland alone, and pretended that he had a claim to the French throne in right of his mother. He had, in reality, no claim at all; but that mattered little in those times. He brought over to his cause many little princes and sovereigns, and even courted the alliance of the people of Flanders—a busy, working community, who had very small respect for kings, and whose head man was a brewer. With such forces as he raised by these means, Edward invaded France; but he did little by that, except run into debt in carrying on the war to the extent of three hundred thousand pounds. The next year he did better; gaining a great sea-fight in the harbour of Sluys. This success, however, was very short-lived, for the Flemings took fright at the siege of Saint Omer and ran away, leaving their weapons and baggage behind them. Philip, the French King, coming up with his army, and Edward being very anxious to decide the war, proposed to settle the difference by single combat with him, or by a fight of one hundred knights on each side. The French King said, he thanked him; but being very well as he was, he would rather not. So, after some skirmishing and talking, a short peace was made.

It was soon broken by King Edward's favoring the cause of John, Earl of Montford; a French nobleman, who asserted a claim of his own against the French King, and offered to do homage to England for the Crown of France, if he could obtain it through England's help. This French lord, himself, was soon defeated by the French King's son, and shut up in a tower in Paris; but his wife, a courageous and beautiful woman, who is said to have had the courage of a man, and the heart of a lion, assembled the people of Brittany, where she then was; and, showing them her infant son, made many pathetic entreaties to them not to desert her and their young Lord. They took fire at this appeal, and rallied around her in the strong castle

of Hennebon. Here she was not only besieged without
by the French under Charles de Blois, but was
endangered within by a dreary old bishop, who was
always representing to the people what horrors they must
undergo if they were faithful—first from famine, and
afterwards from fire and sword. But this noble lady,
whose heart never failed her, encouraged her soldiers
by her own example ; went from post to post like a
great general ; even mounted on horseback fully armed,
and, issuing from the castle by a bye-path, fell upon
the French camp, set fire to the tents, and threw the
whole force into disorder. This done, she got safely
back to Hennebon again, and was received with loud
shouts of joy by the defenders of the castle, who had
given her up for lost. As they were now very short
of provisions, however, and as they could not dine off
enthusiasm, and as the old bishop was always saying,
"I told you what it would come to ! " they began to
lose heart, and to talk of yielding the castle up. The
brave Countess retiring to an upper room and looking
with great grief out to sea, where she expected relief
from England, saw, at this very time, the English ships
in the distance, and was relieved and rescued ! Sir
Walter Manning, the English commander, so admired
her courage, that, being come into the castle with the

English knights, and having made a feast there, he assaulted the French by way of dessert, and beat them off triumphantly. Then he and the knights came back to the castle with great joy; and the Countess who had watched them from a high tower, thanked them with all her heart, and kissed them every one.

This noble lady distinguished herself afterwards in a sea-fight with the French off Guernsey, when she was on her way to England to ask for more troops. Her great spirit roused another lady, the wife of another French lord (whom the French King very barbarously murdered), to distinguish herself scarcely less. The time was fast coming, however, when Edward, Prince of Wales, was to be the great star of this French and English war.

It was in the month of July in the year one thousand three hundred and forty-six, when the King embarked at Southampton for France, with an army of about thirty thousand men in all, attended by the Prince of Wales and by several of the chief nobles. He landed at La Hogue in Normandy; and, burning and destroying as he went, according to custom, advanced up the left bank of the River Seine, and fired the small towns even close to Paris; but, being watched from the right bank of the river by the French King and all his army, it

came to this at last, that Edward found himself, on
Saturday the twenty-sixth of August, one thousand
three hundred and forty-six, on a rising ground behind
the little French village of Crecy, face to face with the
French King's force. And, although the French
King had an enormous army—in number more than
eight times his—he there resolved to beat him or be
beaten.

The young Prince, assisted by the Earl of Oxford
and the Earl of Warwick, led the first division of the
English army; two other great Earls led the second;
and the King, the third. When the morning dawned,
the King received the sacrament, and heard prayers,
and then, mounted on horseback with a white wand in
his hand, rode from company to company, and rank to
rank, cheering and encouraging both officers and men.
Then the whole army breakfasted, each man sitting
on the ground where he had stood; and then they
remained quietly on the ground with their weapons
ready.

Up came the French King with all his great force.
It was dark and angry weather; there was an eclipse
of the sun; there was a thunder-storm, accompanied
with tremendous rain; the frightened birds flew
screaming above the soldiers' heads. A certain captain

in the French army advised the French King, who was
by no means cheerful, not to begin the battle until the
morrow. The King, taking this advice, gave the word
to halt. But, those behind not understanding it, or
desiring to be foremost with the rest, came pressing on.
The roads for a great distance were covered with this
immense army, and with the common people from the
villages, who were flourishing their rude weapons, and
making a great noise. Owing to these circumstances,
the French army advanced in the greatest confusion;
every French lord doing what he liked with his own
men, and putting out the men of every other French
lord.

Now, their King relied strongly upon a great body
of cross-bowmen from Genoa; and these he ordered to
the front to begin the battle, on finding that he could
not stop it. They shouted once, they shouted twice,
they shouted three times, to alarm the English archers;
but, the English archers would have heard them shout
three thousand times and would have never moved.
At last the cross-bowmen went forward a little, and
began to discharge their bolts; upon which, the
English let fly such a hail of arrows, that the Genoese
speedily made off—for their cross-bows, besides being
heavy to carry, required to be wound up with a handle,

and consequently took time to re-load; the English, on the other hand, could discharge their arrows almost as fast as the arrows could fly.

When the French King saw the Genoese turning, he cried out to his men to kill those scoundrels, who were doing harm instead of service. This increased the confusion. Meanwhile the English archers, continuing to shoot as fast as ever, shot down great numbers of the French soldiers and knights; whom certain sly Cornish-men and Welchmen, from the English army, creeping along the ground, despatched with great knives.

The Prince and his division were at this time so hard-pressed, that the Earl of Warwick sent a message to the King, who was overlooking the battle from a windmill, beseeching him to send more aid.

"Is my son killed?" said the King.

"No, sire, please God," returned the messenger.

"Is he wounded?" said the King.

"No, sire."

"Is he thrown to the ground?" said the King.

"No, sire, not so; but, he is very hard-pressed."

"Then," said the King, "go back to those who sent you, and tell them that I shall send no aid; because I set my heart upon my son proving himself this day a brave knight, and because I am resolved, please God, that the honor of a great victory shall be his!"

These bold words, being reported to the Prince and his division, so raised their spirits, that they fought better than ever. The King of France charged gallantly with his men many times; but it was of no use. Night closing in, his horse was killed under him by an English arrow, and the knights and nobles who had clustered thick about him early in the day, were now completely scattered. At last, some of his few remaining followers led him off the field by force, since he would not retire of himself, and they journeyed away to Amiens. The victorious English, lighting their watch-fires, made merry on the field, and the King, riding to meet his gallant son, took him in his arms, kissed him, and told him that he had acted nobly, and proved himself worthy of the day and of the crown. While it was yet night, King Edward was hardly aware of the great victory he had gained; but, next day, it was discovered that eleven princes, twelve hundred knights, and thirty thousand common men, lay dead upon the French side. Among these was the King of Bohemia, an old blind man; who, having been told that his son was wounded in the battle, and

G 2

that no force could stand against the Black Prince, called to him two knights, put himself on horseback between them, fastened the three bridles together, and dashed in among the English, where he was presently slain. He bore as his crest three white ostrich feathers, with the motto *Ich dien*, signifying in English "I serve." This crest and motto were taken by the Prince of Wales in remembrance of that famous day, and have been borne by the Prince of Wales ever since.

Five days after this great battle, the King laid siege to Calais. This siege—ever afterwards memorable—lasted nearly a year. In order to starve the inhabitants out, King Edward built so many wooden houses for the lodgings of his troops, that it is said their quarters looked like a second Calais suddenly sprung up around the first. Early in the siege, the governor of the town drove out what he called the useless mouths, to the number of seventeen hundred persons, men and women, young and old. King Edward allowed them to pass through his lines, and even fed them, and dismissed them with money; but, later in the siege, he was not so merciful—five hundred more, who were afterwards driven out, dying of starvation and misery. The garrison were so hard-pressed at last, that they sent a letter to King Philip, telling him that they had eaten all the horses, all the dogs, and all the rats and mice that could be found in the place; and, that if he did not relieve them, they must either surrender to the English, or eat one another. Philip made one effort to give them relief; but they were so hemmed in by the English power, that he could not succeed, and was fain to leave the place. Upon this they hoisted the English flag and surrendered to King Edward. "Tell your general," said he to the humble messengers who came out of the town, "that I require to have sent here, six of the most distinguished citizens, bare-legged, and in their shirts, with ropes about their necks; and let those six men bring with them the keys of the castle and the town."

When the Governor of Calais related this to the people in the Market-place, there was great weeping and distress; in the midst of which, one worthy citizen, named Eustace de Saint Pierre, rose up and said, that if the six men required were not sacrificed, the whole population would be; therefore, he offered himself as the first. Encouraged by this bright example, five other worthy citizens rose up one after another, and offered themselves to save the rest. The Governor, who was too badly wounded to be able to walk, mounted a poor old horse that had not been eaten, and conducted these good men to the gate, while all the people cried and mourned.

Edward received them wrathfully, and ordered the heads of the whole six to be struck off. Sir Walter Manny pleaded for them, but in vain. However, the good Queen fell upon her knees, and besought the King to give them up to her. The King replied, "I wish you had been somewhere else; but I cannot refuse you." So she had them properly dressed, made a feast for them, and sent them back with a handsome present, to the great rejoicing of the whole camp. I hope the people of Calais loved the daughter to whom she gave birth soon afterwards, for her gentle mother's sake.

Now, came that terrible disease, the Plague, into Europe, hurrying from the heart of China; and killed the wretched people—especially the poor—in such enormous numbers, that one-half of the inhabitants of England are related to have died of it. It killed the cattle, in great numbers, too; and so few working men remained alive, that there were not enough left to till the ground.

After eight years of differing and quarrelling, the Prince of Wales again invaded France with an army of sixty thousand men. He went through the south of the country, burning and plundering wheresoever he went; while his father, who had still the Scottish war upon his hands, did the like in Scotland, but was harassed and worried in his retreat from that country by the Scottish men, who repaid his cruelties with interest.

The French King, Philip, was now dead, and was succeeded by his son John. The Black Prince, called by that name from the colour of the armour he wore to set off his fair complexion, continuing to burn and destroy in France, roused John into determined opposition; and so cruel had the Black Prince been in his campaign, and so severely had the French peasants suffered, that he could not find one who, for love, or money, or the fear of death, would tell him what the French King was doing, or where he was. Thus it happened that he came upon the French King's forces, all of a sudden, near the town of Poictiers, and found that the whole neighbouring country was occupied by a vast French army. "God help us!" said the Black Prince, "we must make the best of it."

So, on a Sunday morning, the eighteenth of September, the Prince—whose army was now reduced to ten thousand men in all—prepared to give battle to the French King, who had sixty thousand horse alone.

While he was so engaged, there came riding from the French camp, a Cardinal, who had persuaded John to let him offer terms, and try to save the shedding of Christian blood. " Save my honour," said the Prince to this good priest, " and save the honour of my army, and I will make any reasonable terms."   He offered to give up all the towns, castles, and prisoners, he had taken, and to swear to make no war in France for seven years ; but, as Philip would hear of nothing but his surrender, with a hundred of his chief knights, the treaty was broken off, and the Prince said, quietly—" God defend the right ; we shall fight to-morrow."

Therefore, on the Monday morning, at break of day the two armies prepared for battle.   The English were posted in a strong place, which could only be approached by one narrow lane, skirted by hedges on both sides. The French attacked them by this lane ; but were so galled and slain by English arrows from behind the hedges, that they were forced to retreat.   Then, went six hundred English bowmen round about, and, coming upon the rear of the French army, rained arrows on them thick and fast.   The French knights, thrown into confusion, quitted their banners and dispersed in all directions.   Said Sir John Chandos to the Prince, " Ride forward, noble Prince, and the day is yours.

The King of France is so valiant a gentleman, that I know he will never fly, and may be taken prisoner." Said the Prince to this, "Advance English banners, in the name of God and St. George!" and on they pressed until they came up with the French King, fighting fiercely with his battle-axe, and, when all his nobles had forsaken him, attended faithfully to the last by his youngest son Philip, only sixteen years of age. Father and son fought well, and the King had already two wounds in his face, and had been beaten down, when he at last delivered himself to a banished French knight, and gave him his right-hand glove in token that he had done so.

The Black Prince was generous as well as brave, and he invited his royal prisoner to supper in his tent, and waited upon him at table, and, when they afterwards rode into London in a gorgeous procession, mounted the French King on a fine cream-coloured horse, and rode at his side on a little pony. This was all very kind, but I think it was, perhaps, a little theatrical too, and has been made more meritorious than it deserved to be; especially as I am inclined to think that the greatest kindness to the King of France would have been not to have shown him to the people at all. However, it must be said, for these acts of politeness, that, in course of time, they did much to soften the horrors of war and the passions of conquerors. It was a long, long time before the common soldiers began to have the benefit of such courtly deeds; but they did at last; and thus it is possible that a poor soldier who asked for quarter at the battle of Waterloo, or any other such great fight, may have owed his life indirectly to Edward the Black Prince.

At this time there stood in the Strand, in London, a palace called the Savoy, which was given up to the captive King of France and his son for their residence. As the King of Scotland had now been King Edward's captive for eleven years too, his success was, at this time, tolerably complete. The Scottish business was settled by the prisoner being released under the title of Sir David, King of Scotland, and by his engaging to pay a large ransom. The state of France encouraged England to propose harder terms to that country, where the people rose against the unspeakable cruelty and barbarity of its nobles; where the nobles rose in turn against the people; where the most frightful outrages were committed on all sides; and where the insurrection of the peasants, called the insurrection of the Jacquerie, from Jacques, a common Christian name among the country people of France, awakened terrors and hatreds that have scarcely yet passed away. A treaty called the Great Peace, was at last signed, under which King Edward agreed to give up the greater part of his conquests, and King John to pay, within six years, a ransom of three million crowns of gold. He was so beset by his own nobles and courtiers for having yielded to these conditions—though they could help him to no better—that he came back of his own will to his old palace-prison of the Savoy, and there died.

There was a Sovereign of Castile at that time, called PEDRO THE CRUEL, who deserved the name remarkably well: having committed, among other cruelties, a variety of murders. This amiable monarch being driven from his throne for his crimes, went to the province of Bourdeaux, where the Black Prince—now married to his cousin JOAN, a pretty widow—was residing, and besought his help. The Prince, who took to him much more kindly than a prince of such fame ought to have taken to such a ruffian, readily listened to his fair promises, and, agreeing to help him, sent secret orders to some troublesome disbanded soldiers of his and his father's, who called themselves the Free Companions, and who had been a pest to the French people for some time, to aid this Pedro. The Prince, himself, going into Spain to head the army of relief, soon set Pedro on his throne again—where he no sooner found himself, than, of course, he behaved like the villain he was, broke his word without the least shame, and abandoned all the promises he had made to the Black Prince.

Now, it had cost the Prince a good deal of money to pay soldiers to support this murderous King; and finding himself, when he came back disgusted to Bourdeaux, not only in bad health, but deeply in debt, he began to tax his French subjects to pay his creditors. They appealed to the French King, CHARLES; war again broke out; and the French town of Limoges, which the Prince had greatly benefited, went over to the French King. Upon this he ravaged the province of which it was the capital; burnt, and plundered, and killed, in the old sickening way; and refused mercy to the prisoners, men, women, and children taken in the offending town, though he was so ill and so much in need of pity himself from Heaven, that he was carried in a litter. He lived to come home and make himself popular with the people and Parliament, and he died on Trinity Sunday, the eighth of June, one thousand three hundred and seventy-six, at forty-six years old.

The whole nation mourned for him as one of the most renowned and beloved princes it had ever had;

and he was buried with great lamentations in Canterbury Cathedral. Near to the tomb of Edward the Confessor, his monument, with his figure, carved in stone, and represented in the old black armour, lying on its back, may be seen at this day, with an ancient coat of mail, a helmet, and a pair of gauntlets hanging from a beam above it, which most people like to believe were once worn by the Black Prince.

King Edward did not outlive his renowned son, long. He was old, and one Alice Perrers, a beautiful lady, had contrived to make him so fond of her in his old age, that he could refuse her nothing, and made himself ridiculous. She little deserved his love, or—what I dare say she valued a great deal more—the jewels of the late Queen, which he gave her among other rich presents. She took the very ring from his finger on the morning of the day when he died, and left him to be pillaged by his faithless servants. Only one good priest was true to him, and attended him to the last.

Besides being famous for the great victories I have related, the reign of King Edward the Third was rendered memorable in better ways, by the growth of architecture and the erection of Windsor Castle. In better ways still, by the rising up of WICKLIFFE, originally a poor parish priest: who devoted himself to

exposing, with wonderful power and success, the ambition and corruption of the Pope, and of the whole
church of which he was the head.

Some of those Flemings were induced to come to
England in this reign too, and to settle in Norfolk,
where they made better woollen cloths than the English
had ever had before. The Order of the Garter (a very
fine thing in its way, but hardly so important as good
clothes for the nation) also dates from this period.
The King is said to have picked up a lady's garter at a
ball, and to have said, *Honi soit qui mal y pense*—in
English, " Evil be to him who evil thinks of it." The
courtiers were usually glad to imitate what the King
said or did, and hence from a slight incident the Order
of the Garter was instituted, and became a great
dignity. So the story goes.

CHAPTER XIX.

ENGLAND UNDER RICHARD THE SECOND.

RICHARD, son of the Black Prince, a boy eleven years of age, succeeded to the Crown under the title of King Richard the Second. The whole English nation were ready to admire him for the sake of his brave father. As to the lords and ladies about the Court, they declared him to be the most beautiful, the wisest, and the best— even of princes—whom the lords and ladies about the Court, generally declare to be the most beautiful, the wisest, and the best of mankind. To flatter a poor boy in this base manner was not a very likely way to develope whatever good was in him; and it brought him to anything but a good or happy end.

The Duke of Lancaster, the young King's uncle— commonly called John of Gaunt, from having been born at Ghent, which the common people so pronounced— was supposed to have some thoughts of the throne himself; but, as he was not popular, and the memory of the Black Prince was, he submitted to his nephew.

The war with France being still unsettled, the Government of England wanted money to provide for the expenses that might arise out of it; accordingly a certain tax, called the Poll-tax, which had originated in the last reign, was ordered to be levied on the people. This was a tax on every person in the kingdom, male and female, above the age of fourteen, of three groats (or three fourpenny pieces) a year; clergymen were charged more, and only beggars were exempt.

I have no need to repeat that the common people of England had long been suffering under great oppression. They were still the mere slaves of the lords of the land on which they lived, and were on most occasions harshly and unjustly treated. But, they had begun by this time to think very seriously of not bearing quite so much; and, probably, were emboldened by that French insurrection I mentioned in the last chapter.

The people of Essex rose against the Poll-tax, and being severely handled by the government officers, killed some of them. At this very time one of the tax-collectors, going his rounds from house to house, at Dartford in Kent, came to the cottage of one WAT, a tiler by trade, and claimed the tax upon his daughter.

Her mother, who was at home, declared that she was under the age of fourteen; upon that, the collector (as other collectors had already done in different parts of England) behaved in a savage way, and brutally insulted Wat Tyler's daughter. The daughter screamed, the mother screamed. Wat the Tiler, who was at work not far off, ran to the spot, and did what any honest father under such provocation might have done—struck the collector dead at a blow.

Instantly the people of that town uprose as one man. They made Wat Tyler their leader; they joined with the people of Essex, who were in arms under a priest called JACK STRAW; they took out of Maidstone prison another priest named JOHN BALL; and gathering in numbers as they went along, advanced, in a great confused army of poor men, to Blackheath. It is said that they wanted to abolish all property, and to declare all men equal. I do not think this very likely; because they stopped the travellers on the roads and made them swear to be true to King Richard and the people. Nor were they at all disposed to injure those who had done them no harm, merely because they were of high station; for, the King's mother, who had to pass through their camp at Blackheath, on her way to her young son, lying for safety in the Tower of London, had merely to kiss a

few dirty-faced rough-bearded men who were noisily
fond of royalty, and so got away in perfect safety. Next
day the whole mass marched on to London Bridge.

There was a drawbridge in the middle, which WILLIAM
WALWORTH the Mayor caused to be raised to prevent
their coming into the city; but they soon terrified the
citizens into lowering it again, and spread themselves,
with great uproar, over the streets. They broke open
the prisons; they burned the papers in Lambeth Palace;
they destroyed the DUKE OF LANCASTER's Palace, the
Savoy, in the Strand, said to be the most beautiful and
splendid in England; they set fire to the books and
documents in the Temple; and made a great riot.
Many of these outrages were committed in drunkenness;
since those citizens, who had well-filled cellars, were
only too glad to throw them open to save the rest of
their property; but even the drunken rioters were very
careful to steal nothing. They were so angry with one
man, who was seen to take a silver cup at the Savoy
Palace and put it in his breast, that they drowned him
in the river, cup and all.

The young King had been taken out to treat with
them before they committed these excesses; but, he and
the people about him were so frightened by the riotous
shouts, that they got back to the Tower in the best way

they could.   This made the insurgents bolder; so they went on rioting away, striking off the heads of those who did not, at a moment's notice, declare for King Richard and the people; and killing as many of the unpopular persons whom they supposed to be their enemies as they could by any means lay hold of.   In this manner they passed one very violent day, and then proclamation was made that the King would meet them at Mile-end, and grant their requests.

The rioters went to Mile-end, to the number of sixty thousand, and the King met them there, and to the King the rioters peaceably proposed four conditions. First, that neither they, nor their children, nor any coming after them, should be made slaves any more. Secondly, that the rent of land should be fixed at a certain price in money, instead of being paid in service. Thirdly, that they should have liberty to buy and sell in all markets and public places, like other free men. Fourthly, that they should be pardoned for past offences. Heaven knows, there was nothing very unreasonable in these proposals!   The young King deceitfully pretended to think so, and kept thirty clerks up, all night, writing out a charter accordingly.

Now, Wat Tyler himself wanted more than this.   He wanted the entire abolition of the forest laws.   He was not at Mile-end with the rest, but, while that meeting was being held, broke into the Tower of London and slew the archbishop and the treasurer, for whose heads the people had cried out loudly the day before. He and his men even thrust their swords into the bed of the Princess of Wales while the Princess was in it, to make certain that none of their enemies were concealed there.

So, Wat and his men still continued armed, and rode about the city. Next morning, the King with a small train of some sixty gentlemen—among whom was WALWORTH the Mayor—rode into Smithfield, and saw Wat and his people at a little distance. Says Wat to his men, "There is the King. I will go speak with him, and tell him what we want."

Straightway Wat rode up to him, and began to talk; "King," says Wat, "dost thou see all my men there?"

"Ah," says the King. "Why?"

"Because," says Wat, "they are all at my command, and have sworn to do whatever I bid them."

Some declared afterwards that as Wat said this, he laid his hand on the King's bridle. Others declared that he was seen to play with his own dagger. I think, myself, that he just spoke to the King like a rough, angry man as he was, and did nothing more. At any rate he was expecting no attack, and preparing for no resistance, when Walworth the Mayor did the not very valiant deed of drawing a short sword and stabbing him in the throat. He dropped from his horse, and one of the King's people speedily finished him. So fell Wat Tyler. Fawners and flatterers made a mighty triumph of it, and set up a cry which will occasionally find an echo to this day. But Wat was a hard-working man, who had suffered much, and had been foully outraged; and it is probable that he was a man of a much higher nature and a much braver spirit than any of the parasites who exulted then, or have exulted since, over his defeat.

Seeing Wat down, his men immediately bent their bows to avenge his fall. If the young King had not had presence of mind at that dangerous moment, both he and the Mayor to boot, might have followed Tyler pretty fast. But, the King riding up to the crowd, cried out that Tyler was a traitor, and that he would be their leader. They were so taken by surprise, that they set up a great shouting and followed the boy until he was met at Islington by a large body of soldiers.

The end of this rising was the then usual end. As soon as the King found himself safe, he unsaid all he had said, and undid all he had done; some fifteen hundred of the rioters were tried (mostly in Essex) with great rigour, and executed with great cruelty. Many of them were hanged on gibbets and left there as a terror to the country people ; and, because their miserable friends took some of the bodies down to bury, the King ordered the rest to be chained up—which was the beginning of the barbarous custom of hanging in chains. The King's falsehood in this business makes such a pitiful figure that I think Wat Tyler appears in history as beyond comparison the truer and more respectable man of the two.

Richard was now sixteen years of age, and married Anne of Bohemia, an excellent princess, who was called " the good Queen Anne." She deserved a better husband ; for the King had been fawned and flattered into a treacherous, wasteful, dissolute, bad young man.

There were two Popes at this time (as if one were not enough !) and their quarrels involved Europe in a great deal of trouble. Scotland was still troublesome too ; and at home there was much jealousy and distrust, and plotting and counter-plotting, because the King feared the ambition of his relations, and particularly of his uncle, the Duke of Lancaster, and the duke had his party against the King, and the King had his party against the duke. Nor were these home troubles

lessened when the duke went to Castile to urge his
claim to the crown of that kingdom; for then the
Duke of Gloucester, another of Richard's uncles,
opposed him, and influenced the Parliament to demand
the dismissal of the King's favorite ministers. The
King said in reply, that he would not for such men
dismiss the meanest servant in his kitchen. But, it
had begun to signify little what a King said when a
Parliament was determined; so Richard was at last
obliged to give way, and to agree to another Government of the kingdom, under a commission of fourteen
nobles for a year. His uncle of Gloucester was at the
head of this commission, and, in fact, appointed everybody composing it.

Having done all this, the King declared as soon as
he saw an opportunity that he had never meant to do it,
and that it was all illegal; and he got the judges
secretly to sign a declaration to that effect. The secret
oozed out directly, and was carried to the Duke of
Gloucester. The Duke of Gloucester, at the head of
forty thousand men, met the King on his entering into
London to enforce his authority; the King was helpless
against him; his favorites and ministers were impeached and were mercilessly executed. Among them
were two men whom the people regarded with very

different feelings; one, Robert Tresilian, Chief Justice, who was hated for having made what was called "the bloody circuit" to try the rioters; the other, Sir Simon Burley, an honourable knight, who had been the dear friend of the Black Prince, and the governor and guardian of the King. For this gentleman's life the good Queen even begged of Gloucester on her knees; but Gloucester (with or without reason) feared and hated him, and replied, that if she valued her husband's crown, she had better beg no more. All this was done under what was called by some the wonderful—and by others, with better reason, the merciless—Parliament.

But Gloucester's power was not to last for ever. He held it for only a year longer; in which year the famous battle of Otterbourne, sung in the old ballad of Chevy Chase, was fought. When the year was out, the King, turning suddenly to Gloucester, in the midst of a great council said, "Uncle, how old am I?" "Your highness," returned the Duke, "is in your twenty-second year." "Am I so much?" said the King, "then I will manage my own affairs! I am much obliged to you, my good lords, for your past services, but I need them no more." He followed this up, by appointing a new Chancellor and a new Treasurer, and announced to the people that he had resumed the Government. He held it for eight years without opposition. Through all that time, he kept his determination to revenge himself some day upon his uncle Gloucester, in his own breast.

At last the good Queen died, and then the King, desiring to take a second wife, proposed to his council that he should marry Isabella, of France, the daughter of Charles the Sixth: who, the French courtiers said (as the English courtiers had said of Richard), was a marvel of beauty and wit, and quite a phenomenon— of seven years old. The council were divided about this marriage, but it took place. It secured peace between England and France for a quarter of a century; but it was strongly opposed to the prejudices of the English people. The Duke of Gloucester, who was anxious to take the occasion of making himself popular, declaimed against it loudly, and this at length decided the King to execute the vengeance he had been nursing so long.

He went with a gay company to the Duke of Gloucester's house, Pleshey Castle, in Essex, where the Duke, suspecting nothing, came out into the court-yard to receive his royal visitor. While the King conversed in a friendly manner with the Duchess, the Duke was quietly seized, hurried away, shipped for

Calais, and lodged in the castle there. His friends, the Earls of Arundel and Warwick, were taken in the same treacherous manner, and confined to their castles. A few days after, at Nottingham, they were impeached of high treason. The Earl of Arundel was condemned and beheaded, and the Earl of Warwick was banished. Then, a writ was sent by a messenger to the Governor of Calais, requiring him to send the Duke of Gloucester over to be tried. In three days he returned an answer that he could not do that, because the Duke of Gloucester had died in prison. The Duke was declared a traitor, his property was confiscated to the King, a real or pretended confession he had made in prison to one of the Justices of the Common Pleas was produced against him, and there was an end of the matter. How the unfortunate duke died, very few cared to know. Whether he really died naturally; whether he killed himself; whether, by the King's order, he was strangled, or smothered between two beds (as a serving-man of the Governor's named Hall, did afterwards declare), cannot be discovered. There is not much doubt that he was killed, somehow or other, by his nephew's orders. Among the most active nobles in these proceedings were the King's cousin, Henry Bolingbroke, whom the King had made Duke of

Hereford to smooth down the old family quarrels, and some others: who had in the family-plotting times done just such acts themselves as they now condemned in the duke. They seem to have been a corrupt set of men; but such men were easily found about the court in such days.

The people murmured at all this, and were still very sore about the French marriage. The nobles saw how little the King cared for law, and how crafty he was, and began to be somewhat afraid for themselves. The King's life was a life of continued feasting and excess; his retinue, down to the meanest servants, were dressed in the most costly manner, and caroused at his tables, it is related, to the number of ten thousand persons every day. He himself, surrounded by a body of ten thousand archers, and enriched by a duty on wool which the Commons had granted to him for life, saw no danger of ever being otherwise than powerful and absolute, and was as fierce and haughty as a King could be.

He had two of his old enemies left, in the persons of the Dukes of Hereford and Norfolk. Sparing these no more than the others, he tampered with the Duke of Hereford until he got him to declare before the Council that the Duke of Norfolk had lately held some treasonable talk with him, as he was riding near

Brentford; and that he had told him, among other things, that he could not believe the King's oath —which nobody could, I should think. For this treachery he obtained a pardon, and the Duke of Norfolk was summoned to appear and defend himself. As he denied the charge and said his accuser was a liar and a traitor, both noblemen, according to the manner of those times, were held in custody, and the truth was ordered to be decided by wager of battle at Coventry. This wager of battle meant that whosoever won the combat was to be considered in the right; which nonsense meant in effect, that no strong man could ever be wrong. A great holiday was made; a great crowd assembled, with much parade and show; and the two combatants were about to rush at each other with their lances, when the King, sitting in a pavilion to see fair, threw down the truncheon he carried in his hand, and forbade the battle. The Duke of Hereford was to be banished for ten years, and the Duke of Norfolk was to be banished for life. So said the King. The Duke of Hereford went to France, and went no farther. The Duke of Norfolk made a pilgrimage to the Holy Land, and afterwards died at Venice of a broken heart.

Faster and fiercer, after this, the King went on in

his career. The Duke of Lancaster, who was the father of the Duke of Hereford, died soon after the departure of his son; and, the King, although he had solemnly granted to that son leave to inherit his father's property, if it should come to him during his banishment, immediately seized it all, like a robber. The judges were so afraid of him, that they disgraced themselves by declaring this theft to be just and lawful. His avarice knew no bounds. He outlawed seventeen counties at once, on a frivolous pretence, merely to raise money by way of fines for misconduct. In short, he did as many dishonest things as he could; and cared so little for the discontent of his subjects—though even the spaniel favorites began to whisper to him that there was such a thing as discontent afloat—that he took that time, of all others, for leaving England and making an expedition against the Irish.

He was scarcely gone, leaving the DUKE OF YORK Regent in his absence, when his cousin, Henry of Hereford, came over from France to claim the rights of which he had been so monstrously deprived. He was immediately joined by the two great Earls of Northumberland and Westmoreland; and his uncle the Regent, finding the King's cause unpopular, and the disinclination of the army to act against Henry,

very strong, withdrew with the royal forces towards
Bristol. Henry, at the head of an army, came from
Yorkshire (where he had landed) to London and
followed him. They joined their forces—how they
brought that about, is not distinctly understood—and
proceeded to Bristol Castle, whither three noblemen
had taken the young Queen. The castle surrendering,
they presently put those three noblemen to death.
The Regent then remained there, and Henry went on
to Chester.

All this time, the boisterous weather had prevented
the King from receiving intelligence of what had
occurred. At length it was conveyed to him in Ireland, and he sent over the EARL OF SALISBURY, who,
landing at Conway, rallied the Welshmen, and waited
for the King a whole fortnight; at the end of that time
the Welshmen, who were perhaps not very warm for
him in the beginning, quite cooled down, and went
home. When the King did land on the Coast at last,
he came with a pretty good power, but his men cared
nothing for him and quickly deserted. Supposing the
Welshmen to be still at Conway, he disguised himself
as a priest, and made for that place in company with
his two brothers and some few of their adherents. But,
there were no Welshmen left—only Salisbury and a

hundred soldiers. In this distress, the King's two brothers, Exeter and Surrey, offered to go to Henry to learn what his intentions were. Surrey, who was true to Richard, was put into prison. Exeter, who was false, took the royal badge, which was a hart, off his shield, and assumed the rose, the badge of Henry. After this, it was pretty plain to the King what Henry's intentions were, without sending any more messengers to ask.

The fallen King, thus deserted—hemmed in on all sides, and pressed with hunger—rode here and rode there, and went to this castle, and went to that castle, endeavouring to obtain some provisions, but could find none. He rode wretchedly back to Conway, and there surrendered himself to the Earl of Northumberland, who came from Henry, in reality to take him prisoner, but in appearance to offer terms ; and whose men were hidden not far off. By this earl he was conducted to the castle of Flint, where his cousin, Henry, met him, and dropped on his knee as if he were still respectful to his sovereign.

"Fair cousin of Lancaster," said the King, "you are very welcome " (very welcome, no doubt ; but he would have been more so, in chains or without a head.)

" My lord," replied Henry, " I am come a little

before my time; but, with your good pleasure, I will
show you the reason. Your people complain with
some bitterness, that you have ruled them rigorously
for two-and-twenty years. Now, if it please God, I
will help you to govern them better in future."

"Fair cousin," replied the abject King, "since it
pleaseth you, it pleaseth me mightily."

After this, the trumpets sounded, and the King was
stuck on a wretched horse, and carried prisoner to
Chester, where he was made to issue a proclamation,
calling a Parliament. From Chester he was taken on
towards London. At Lichfield he tried to escape by
getting out of a window and letting himself down into
a garden; it was all in vain, however, and he was
carried on and shut up in the Tower, where no one
pitied him, and where the whole people, whose patience
he had quite tired out, reproached him without mercy.
Before he got there, it is related, that his very dog left
him and departed from his side to lick the hand of
Henry.

The day before the Parliament met, a deputation
went to this wrecked King, and told him that he had
promised the Duke of Northumberland at Conway
Castle to resign the crown. He said he was quite
ready to do it, and signed a paper in which he

renounced his authority and absolved his people from their allegiance to him. He had so little spirit left that he gave his royal ring to his triumphant cousin Henry with his own hand, and said, that if he could have had leave to appoint a successor, that same Henry was the man of all others whom he would have named. Next day, the Parliament assembled in Westminster Hall, where Henry sat at the side of the throne, which was empty and covered with a cloth of gold. The paper just signed by the King was read to the multitude amid shouts of joy, which were echoed through all the streets; when some of the noise had died away, the King was formally deposed. Then Henry arose, and, making the sign of the cross on his forehead and breast, challenged the realm of England as his right; the archbishops of Canterbury and York seated him on the throne.

The multitude shouted again, and the shouts re-echoed throughout all the streets. No one remembered, now, that Richard the Second had ever been the most beautiful, the wisest, and the best of princes; and he now made living (to my thinking) a far more sorry spectacle in the Tower of London, than Wat Tyler had made, lying dead, among the hoofs of the royal horses in Smithfield.

The Poll-tax died with Wat. The Smiths to the King and Royal Family, could make no chains in which the King could hang the people's recollection of him; so the Poll-tax was never collected.

CHAPTER XX.

ENGLAND UNDER HENRY THE FOURTH,

CALLED, BOLINGBROKE.

DURING the last reign, the preaching of Wickliffe against the pride and cunning of the Pope and all his men, had made a great noise in England. Whether the new King wished to be in favour with the priests, or whether he hoped, by pretending to be very religious, to cheat Heaven itself into the belief that he was not an usurper, I don't know. Both suppositions are likely enough. It is certain that he began his reign by making a strong show against the followers of Wickcliffe, who were called Lollards, or heretics — although his father, John of Gaunt, had been of that way of thinking, as he himself had been more than suspected of being. It is no less certain that he first established in England the detestable and atrocious custom, brought from abroad, of burning those people as a punishment for their opinions. It was the importation into England of one of the practices of what was called the Holy Inquisition: which was the most *unholy* and the most infamous tribunal that ever disgraced mankind, and made men more like demons than followers of Our Saviour.

No real right to the crown, as you know, was in this King. Edward Mortimer, the young Earl of March—who was only eight or nine years old, and who was descended from the Duke of Clarence, the elder brother of Henry's father—was, by succession, the real heir to the throne. However, the King got his son declared Prince of Wales; and, obtaining possession of the young Earl of March and his little brother, kept them in confinement (but not severely) in Windsor Castle. He then required the Parliament to decide what was to be done with the deposed King, who was quiet enough, and who only said that he hoped his cousin Henry would be "a good lord" to him. The Parliament replied that they would recommend his being kept in some secret place where the people could not resort, and where his friends should not be admitted to see him. Henry accordingly passed this sentence upon him, and it now began to be pretty clear to the nation that Richard the Second would not live very long.

It was a noisy Parliament, as it was an unprincipled one, and the Lords quarrelled so violently among themselves as to which of them had been loyal and which disloyal, and which consistent and which inconsistent, that forty gauntlets are said to have been thrown upon the floor at one time as challenges to as many battles: the truth being that they were all false and base together, and had been, at one time with the old King, and at another time with the new one, and seldom true for any length of time to any one. They soon began to plot again. A conspiracy was formed to invite the King to a tournament at Oxford, and then to take him by surprise and kill him. This murderous enterprise, which was agreed upon at secret meetings in the house of the Abbot of Westminster, was betrayed by the Earl of Rutland—one of the conspirators. The King, instead of going to the tournament or staying at Windsor (where the conspirators suddenly went, on finding themselves discovered, with the hope of seizing him), retired to London, proclaimed them all traitors, and advanced upon them with a great force. They retired into the west of England, proclaiming Richard King; but, the people rose against them, and they were all slain. Their treason hastened the death of the deposed monarch. Whether he was

killed by hired assassins, or whether he was starved
to death, or whether he refused food on hearing of his
brothers being killed (who were in that plot) is very
doubtful. He met his death somehow; and his body
was publicly shown at St. Paul's Cathedral with only
the lower part of the face uncovered. I can scarcely
doubt that he was killed by the King's orders.

The French wife of the miserable Richard was now
only ten years old; and, when her father, Charles of
France, heard of her misfortunes and of her lonely
condition in England, he went mad: as he had several
times done before, during the last five or six years.
The French Dukes of Burgundy and Bourbon took
up the poor girl's cause, without caring much about it,
but on the chance of getting something out of England.
The people of Bourdeaux, who had a sort of superstitious attachment to the memory of Richard, because
he was born there, swore by the Lord that he had
been the best man in all his kingdom—which was
going rather far—and promised to do great things
against the English. Nevertheless, when they came
to consider that they, and the whole people of France,
were ruined by their own nobles, and that the English
rule was much the better of the two, they cooled down
again; and the two dukes, although they were very

great men, could do nothing without them. Then,
began negociations between France and England for
the sending home to Paris of the poor little Queen
with all her jewels and her fortune of two hundred
thousand francs in gold. The King was quite willing
to restore the young lady, and even the jewels; but
he said he really could not part with the money. So,
at last she was safely deposited at Paris without her
fortune, and then the Duke of Burgundy (who was
cousin to the French King) began to quarrel with the
Duke of Orleans (who was brother to the French King)
about the whole matter; and those two dukes made
France even more wretched than ever.

As the idea of conquering Scotland was still popular
at home, the King marched to the river Tyne and demanded homage of the King of that country. This being
refused, he advanced to Edinburgh, but did little there;
for, his army being in want of provisions, and the Scotch
being very careful to hold him in check without giving
battle, he was obliged to retire. It is to his immortal
honour that in this sally he burnt no villages and
slaughtered no people, but was particularly careful that
his army should be merciful and harmless. It was a
great example in those ruthless times.

A war among the border people of England and

Scotland went on for twelve months, and then the Earl of Northumberland, the nobleman who had helped Henry to the crown, began to rebel against him— probably because nothing that Henry could do for him would satisfy his extravagant expectations.   There was a certain Welsh gentleman, named OWEN GLENDOWER, who had been a student in one of the Inns of Court, and had afterwards been in the service of the late King, whose Welsh property was taken from him by a powerful lord related to the present King, who was his neighbour. Appealing for redress, and getting none, he took up arms, was made an outlaw, and declared himself sovereign of Wales.   He pretended to be a magician; and not only were the Welsh people stupid enough to believe him, but, even Henry believed him too; for, making three expeditions into Wales, and being three times driven back by the wildness of the country, the bad weather, and the skill of Glendower, he thought he was defeated by the Welshman's magic arts.   However, he took Lord Grey and Sir Edmund Mortimer, prisoners, and allowed the relatives of Lord Grey to ransom him, but would not extend such favour to Sir Edmund Mortimer.   Now, Henry Percy, called HOTSPUR, son of the Earl of Northumberland, who was married to Mortimer's sister, is supposed to have taken offence at this; and, therefore, in conjunction with his father and some others, to have joined Owen Glendower, and risen against Henry.   It is by no means clear that this was the real cause of the conspiracy; but perhaps it was made the pretext.   It was formed, and was very powerful; including SCROOP, Archbishop of York, and the EARL OF DOUGLAS, a powerful and brave Scottish nobleman.   The King was prompt and active, and the two armies met at Shrewsbury.

There were about fourteen thousand men in each. The old Earl of Northumberland being sick, the rebel forces were led by his son.   The King wore plain armour to deceive the enemy; and four noblemen, with the same object, wore the royal arms.   The rebel charge was so furious, that every one of those gentlemen was killed, the royal standard was beaten down, and the young Prince of Wales was severely wounded in the face.   But, he was one of the bravest and best soldiers that ever lived, and he fought so well, and the King's troops were so encouraged by his bold example, that they rallied immediately, and cut the enemy's forces all to pieces.   Hotspur was killed by an arrow in the brain, and the rout was so complete that the whole rebellion was struck down by this one blow.   The Earl of Northumberland surrendered himself soon after hearing of the death of his son, and received a pardon for all his offences.

There were some lingerings of rebellion yet : Owen Glendower being retired to Wales, and a preposterous story being spread among the ignorant people that King Richard was still alive.   How they could have believed such nonsense it is difficult to imagine; but they certainly did suppose that the Court fool of the late King, who was something like him, was he, himself ; so that it seemed as if, after giving so much trouble to the country in his life, he was still to trouble it after his death.   This was not the worst.   The young Earl of March and his brother were stolen out of Windsor castle.   Being retaken, and being found to have been spirited away by one Lady Spencer, she accused her own brother, that Earl of Rutland who was in the former conspiracy and was now Duke of York, of being in the plot.   For this he was ruined in fortune, though not put to death ; and then another plot arose among the old Earl of Northumberland, some other lords, and that same Scroop, Archbishop of York, who was with the rebels before.   These conspirators caused a writing to be posted on the church doors, accusing the King of a variety of crimes ; but, the King being eager and vigilant to oppose them, they were all taken, and the Archbishop was executed. This was the first time that a great churchman had been slain by the law in England; but the King was resolved that it should be done, and done it was.

The next most remarkable event of this time was the seizure, by Henry, of the heir to the Scottish throne— James, a boy of nine years old. He had been put aboard-ship by his father, the Scottish King Robert, to save him from the designs of his uncle, when, on his way to France, he was accidentally taken by some English cruisers. He remained a prisoner in England for nineteen years, and became in his prison a student and a famous poet.

With the exception of occasional troubles with the Welch and with the French, the rest of King Henry's reign was quiet enough. But, the King was far from happy, and probably was troubled in his conscience by knowing that he had usurped the crown, and had occasioned the death of his miserable cousin. The Prince of Wales, though brave and generous, is said to have been wild and dissipated, and even to have drawn his sword on GASCOIGNE, the Chief Justice of the King's Bench, because he was firm in dealing impartially with one of his dissolute companions. Upon this the Chief Justice is said to have ordered him immediately to prison; the Prince of Wales is said to have submitted with a good grace; and the King is said to have exclaimed, "Happy is the monarch who has so just a judge, and a son so willing to obey the laws." This is all very doubtful, and so is another story (of which Shakespeare has made beautiful use), that the Prince once took the crown out of his father's chamber as he was sleeping, and tried it on his own head.

The King's health sank more and more, he became subject to violent eruptions on the face and to bad epileptic fits, and his spirits sank every day. At last, as he was praying before the shrine of St. Edward at Westminster Abbey, he was seized with a terrible fit, and was carried into the Abbot's chamber, where he presently died. It had been foretold that he would die at Jerusalem, which certainly is not, and certainly never was, Westminster. But, as the Abbot's room had long been called the Jerusalem chamber, people said it was all the same thing, and were quite satisfied with the prediction.

This King died on the 20th of March, 1413, in the forty-seventh year of his age, and the fourteenth of his reign. He was buried in Canterbury Cathedral. He had been twice married, and had, by his first wife, a family of four sons and two daughters. Considering his duplicity before he came to the throne, his unjust seizure of it, and, above all, his making that monstrous law for the burning of what the priests called heretics, he was a reasonably good King, as kings went.

CHAPTER XXI.

ENGLAND UNDER HENRY THE FIFTH.

FIRST PART.

THE Prince of Wales began his reign like a generous
and honest man. He set the young Earl of March,
free ; he restored their estates and their honours to the
Percy family, who had lost them by their rebellion
against his father ; he ordered the imbecile and unfortunate Richard to be honourably buried among the
Kings of England; and he dismissed all his wild companions, with assurances that they should not want, if
they would resolve to be steady, faithful, and true.

It is much easier to burn men than to burn their
opinions; and those of the Lollards were spreading
every day. The Lollards were represented by the
priests—probably false for the most part—to entertain
treasonable designs against the new King; and Henry,
suffering himself to be worked upon by these repre-

sentations, sacrificed his friend Sir John Oldcastle, the Lord Cobham to them, after trying in vain to convert him by arguments. He was declared guilty, as the head of the sect, and sentenced to the flames ; but, he escaped from the Tower before the day of execution (postponed for fifty days by the King himself), and summoned the Lollards to meet him near London on a certain day. So the priests told the King, at least. I doubt whether there was any conspiracy beyond such as was got up by their agents. On the day appointed, instead of five-and-twenty thousand men, under the command of Sir John Oldcastle, in the meadows of St. Giles, the King found only eighty men, and no Sir John at all. There was, in another place, an addle-headed brewer, who had gold trappings to his horses, and a pair of gilt spurs in his breast—expecting to be made a knight next day by Sir John, and so to gain the right to wear them—but there was no Sir John, nor did anybody give any information respecting him, though the King offered great rewards for such intelligence. Thirty of these unfortunate Lollards were hanged and drawn immediately, and were then burnt, gallows and all ; and the various prisons in and around London were crammed full of others. Some of these unfortu-nate men made various confessions of treasonable designs; but, such confessions were easily got, under torture and the fear of fire, and are very little to be trusted. To finish the sad story of Sir John Oldcastle at once, I may mention that he escaped into Wales, and remained there safely, for four years. When discovered by Lord Powis, it is very doubtful if he would have been taken alive—so great was the old soldier's bravery—if a miserable old woman had not come behind him and broken his legs with a stool. He was carried to London in a horse-litter, was fastened by an iron chain to a gibbet,' and so roasted to death.

To make the state of France as plain as I can in a few words, I should tell you that the Duke of Orleans, and the Duke of Burgundy, commonly called "John without fear," had had a grand reconciliation of their quarrel in the last reign, and had appeared to be in quite a heavenly state of mind. Immediately after which, on a Sunday, in the public streets of Paris, the Duke of Orleans was murdered by a party of twenty men, set on by the Duke of Burgundy—according to his own deliberate confession. The widow of King Richard had been married in France to the eldest son of the Duke of Orleans. The poor mad King was quite powerless to help his daughter, and the Duke of Burgundy became the real master

of France. Isabella dying, her husband (Duke of
Orleans since the death of his father) married the
daughter of the Count of Armagnac, who, being a much
abler man than his young son-in-law, headed his party;
thence called after him Armagnacs. Thus, France
was now in this terrible condition, that it had in it the
party of the King's son, the Dauphin Louis; the party
of the Duke of Burgundy, who was the father of
the Dauphin's ill-used wife; and the party of the
Armagnacs; all hating each other; all fighting
together; all composed of the most depraved nobles that
the earth has ever known; and all tearing unhappy
France to pieces.

The late King had watched these dissensions from
England, sensible (like the French people) that no
enemy of France could injure her more than her
own nobility. The present King now advanced a
claim to the French throne. His demand being, of
course, refused, he reduced his proposal to a certain
large amount of French territory, and to demanding
the French princess, Catherine, in marriage with a
fortune of two millions of golden crowns. He was
offered less territory and fewer crowns, and no princess;
but he called his ambassadors home and prepared for
war. Then, he proposed to take the princess with one

million of crowns. The French Court replied that he
should have the princess with two hundred thousand
crowns less ; he said this would not do (he had never
seen the princess in his life), and assembled his army
at Southampton. There was a short plot at home just at
that time, for deposing him, and making the Earl of March
king ; but, the conspirators were all speedily condemned
and executed, and the King embarked for France.

It is dreadful to observe how long a bad example
will be followed ; but, it is encouraging to know that a
good example is never thrown away. The King's first
act on disembarking at the mouth of the river Seine,
three miles from Harfleur, was to imitate his father,
and to proclaim his solemn orders that the lives and
property of the peaceable inhabitants should be
respected on pain of death. It is agreed by French
writers, to his lasting renown, that even while his
soldiers were suffering the greatest distress from want
of food, these commands were rigidly obeyed.

With an army in all of thirty thousand men, he
besieged the town of Harfleur both by sea and land for
five weeks ; at the end of which time the town surrendered, and the inhabitants were allowed to depart
with only five-pence each, and a part of their clothes.
All the rest of their possessions was divided amongst

the English army. But, that army suffered so much, in spite of its successes, from disease and privation, that it was already reduced one half. Still, the King was determined not to retire until he had struck a greater blow. Therefore, against the advice of all his counsellors, he moved on with his little force towards Calais. When he came up to the river Somme he was unable to cross, in consequence of the ford being fortified ; and, as the English moved up the left bank of the river looking for a crossing, the French, who had broken all the bridges, moved up the right bank, watching them, and waiting to attack them when they should try to pass it. At last the English found a crossing and got safely over. The French held a council of war at Rouen, resolved to give the English battle, and sent heralds to King Henry to know by which road he was going. " By the road that will take me straight to Calais!" said the King, and sent them away with a present of a hundred crowns.

The English moved on, until they beheld the French, and then the King gave orders to form in line of battle. The French not coming on, the army broke up after remaining in battle array till night, and got good rest and refreshment at a neighbouring village. The French were now all lying in another village, through which they knew the English must pass. They were resolved that the English should begin the battle. The English had no means of retreat, if their King had had any such intention ; and so the two armies passed the night, close together.

To understand these armies well, you must bear in mind that the immense French army had, among its notable persons, almost the whole of that wicked nobility, whose debauchery had made France a desert ; and so besotted were they by pride, and by contempt for the common people, that they had scarcely any bowmen (if indeed they had any at all) in their whole enormous number : which, compared with the English army, was at least 'as six to one. For these proud fools had said that the bow was not a fit weapon for knightly hands, and that France must be defended by gentlemen only. We shall see, presently, what hand the gentlemen made of it.

Now, on the English side, among the little force, there was a good proportion of men who were not gentlemen by any means, but who were good stout archers for all that. Among them, in the morning— having slept little at night, while the French were carousing and making sure of victory—the King rode, on a grey horse ; wearing on his head a helmet of shining steel, surmounted by a crown of gold, sparkling with precious stones; and bearing over his armour, embroidered together, the arms of England and the arms of France. The archers looked at the shining helmet and the crown of gold and the sparkling jewels, and admired them all; but, what they admired most was the King's cheerful face, and his bright blue eye, as he told them that, for himself, he had made up his mind to conquer there or to die there, and that England should never have a ransom to pay for *him*. There was one brave knight who chanced to say that he wished some of the many gallant gentlemen and good soldiers, who were then idle at home in England, were there to increase their numbers. But the King told him that, for his part, he did not wish for one more man. "The fewer we have," said he, "the greater will be the honor we shall win!" His men, being now all in good heart, were refreshed with bread and wine, and heard prayers, and waited quietly for the French. The King waited for the French, because they were drawn up thirty deep (the little English force was only three deep) on very difficult and heavy ground; and he knew that when they moved, there must be confusion among them.

As they did not move, he sent off two parties :—one,

to lie concealed in a wood on the left of the French: the other, to set fire to some houses behind the French after the battle should be begun. This was scarcely done, when three of the proud French gentlemen, who were to defend their country without any help from the base peasants, came riding out, calling upon the English to surrender. The King warned those gentlemen himself to retire with all speed if they cared for their lives, and ordered the English banners to advance. Upon that, Sir Thomas Erpingham, a great English general, who commanded the archers, threw his truncheon into the air, joyfully; and all the English men, kneeling down upon the ground and biting it as if they took possession of the country, rose up with a great shout and fell upon the French.

Every archer was furnished with a great stake tipped with iron; and his orders were, to thrust this stake into the ground, to discharge his arrow, and then to fall back, when the French horsemen came on. As the haughty French gentlemen, who were to break the English archers and utterly destroy them with their knightly lances, came riding up, they were received with such a blinding storm of arrows, that they broke and turned. Horses and men rolled over one another, and the confusion was terrific. Those who rallied and charged the archers got among the stakes on slippery and boggy ground, and were so bewildered that the English archers—who wore no armour and even took off their leathern coats to be more active—cut them to pieces, root and branch. Only three French horsemen got within the stakes, and those were instantly despatched. All this time the dense French army, being in armour, were sinking knee-deep into the mire; while the light English archers, half-naked, were as fresh and active as if they were fighting on a marble floor.

But now, the second division of the French coming to the relief of the first, closed up in a firm mass; the English, headed by the King, attacked them; and the deadliest part of the battle began. The King's brother, the Duke of Clarence, was struck down, and numbers of the French surrounded him; but, King Henry, standing over the body, fought like a lion until they were beaten off.

Presently, came up a band of eighteen French knights, bearing the banner of a certain French lord, who had sworn to kill or take the English King. One of them struck him such a blow with a battle-axe that he reeled and fell upon his knees; but, his faithful

men, immediately closing round him, killed every one
of those eighteen knights, and so that French lord
never kept his oath.

The French Duke of Alençon, seeing this, made a
desperate charge, and cut his way close up to the
Royal Standard of England.   He beat down the Duke
of York, who was standing near it; and, when the
King came to his rescue, struck off a piece of the
crown he wore.   But, he never struck another blow
in this world; for, even as he was in the act of saying
who he was, and that he surrendered to the King;
and even as the King stretched out his hand to give
him a safe and honorable acceptance of the offer; he
fell dead, pierced by innumerable wounds.

The death of this nobleman decided the battle.   The
third division of the French army, which had never
struck a blow yet, and which was, in itself, more than
double the whole English power, broke and fled.   At
this time of the fight, the English, who as yet had
made no prisoners, began to take them in immense
numbers, and were still occupied in doing so, or in
killing those who would not surrender, when a great
noise arose in the rear of the French—their flying
banners were seen to stop—and King Henry, supposing
a great reinforcement to have arrived, gave orders that

all the prisoners should be put to death. As soon, however, as it was found that the noise was only occasioned by a body of plundering peasants, the terrible massacre was stopped.

Then King Henry called to him the French herald, and asked him to whom the victory belonged.

The herald replied, "To the King of England."

"*We* have not made this havoc and slaughter," said the King. "It is the wrath of Heaven on the sins of France. What is the name of that castle yonder?"

The herald answered him, "My lord, it is the castle of Azincourt."

Said the King, "From henceforth this battle shall be known to posterity, by the name of the battle of Azincourt."

Our English historians have made it Agincourt; but, under that name, it will ever be famous in English annals.

The loss upon the French side was enormous. Three Dukes were killed, two more were taken prisoners, seven Counts were killed, three more were taken prisoners, and ten thousand knights and gentlemen were slain upon the field. The English loss amounted to sixteen hundred men, among whom were the Duke of York and the Earl of Suffolk.

War is a dreadful thing; and it is appalling to know how the English were obliged, next morning, to kill those prisoners mortally wounded, who yet writhed in agony upon the ground; how the dead upon the French side were stripped by their own countrymen and countrywomen, and afterwards buried in great pits; how the dead upon the English side were piled up in a great barn, and how their bodies and the barn were all burned together.   It is in such things, and in many more much too horrible to relate, that the real desolation and wickedness of war consist.   Nothing can make war otherwise than horrible.   But the dark side of it was little thought of and soon forgotten; and it cast no shade of trouble on the English people, except on those who had lost friends or relations in the fight. They welcomed their King home with shouts of rejoicing, and plunged into the water to bear him ashore on their shoulders, and flocked out in crowds to welcome him in every town through which he passed, and hung rich carpets and tapestries out of the windows, and strewed the streets with flowers, and made the fountains run with wine, as the great field of Agincourt had run with blood.

SECOND PART.

THAT proud and wicked French nobility who dragged their country to destruction, and who were every day and every year regarded with deeper hatred and detestation in the hearts of the French people, learnt nothing, even from the defeat of Agincourt. So far from uniting against the common enemy, they became, among themselves, more violent, more bloody, and more false—if that were possible—than they had been before. The Count of Armagnac persuaded the French king to plunder of her treasures Queen Isabella of Bavaria, and to make her a prisoner. She, who had hitherto been the bitter enemy of the Duke of Burgundy, proposed to join him, in revenge. He attacked her guards and carried her off to Troyes, where she proclaimed herself Regent of France, and made him her lieutenant. The Armagnac party were at that time possessed of Paris; but, one of the gates of the

city being secretly opened on a certain night to a
party of the duke's men, they got into Paris, threw
into the prisons all the Armagnacs upon whom they
could lay their hands, and, a few nights afterwards,
with the aid of a furious mob of sixty thousand people,
broke the prisons open, and killed them all. The
former Dauphin was now dead, and the king's third
son bore the title. Him, in the height of this murderous scene, a French knight hurried out of bed,
wrapt in a sheet, and bore away to Poitiers. So, when
the revengeful Isabella and the Duke of Burgundy
entered Paris in triumph after the slaughter of their
enemies, the Dauphin was proclaimed at Poitiers as
the real Regent.

King Henry had not been idle since his victory of
Agincourt, but had repulsed a brave attempt of the
French to recover Harfleur; had gradually conquered
a great part of Normandy; and, at this crisis of affairs,
took the important town of Rouen, after a siege of half
a year. This great loss so alarmed the French, that
the Duke of Burgundy proposed that a meeting to
treat of peace should be held between the French and
the English kings in a plain by the river Seine. On the
appointed day, King Henry appeared there, with his
two brothers, Clarence and Gloucester, and a thousand

men.   The unfortunate French King, being more mad than usual that day, could not come; but, the Queen came, and with her the Princess Catherine : who was a very lovely creature, and who made a real impression on King Henry, now that he saw her for the first time. This was the most important circumstance that arose out of the meeting.

As if it were impossible for a French nobleman of that time to be true to his word of honor in anything, Henry discovered that the Duke of Burgundy was, at that very moment, in secret treaty with the Dauphin ; and he therefore abandoned the negociation.

The Duke of Burgundy and the Dauphin, each of whom with the best reason distrusted the other as a noble ruffian surrounded by a party of noble ruffians, were rather at a loss how to proceed after this; but, at length they agreed to meet, on a bridge over the river Yonne, where it was arranged that there should be two strong gates put up, with an empty space between them ; and that the Duke of Burgundy should come into that space by one gate, with ten men only ; and that the Dauphin should come into that space by the other gate, also with ten men, and no more.

So far the Dauphin kept his word, but no farther. When the Duke of Burgundy was on his knee before him in the act of speaking, one of the Dauphin's noble ruffians cut the said duke down with a small axe, and others speedily finished him.

It was in vain for the Dauphin to pretend that this base murder was not done with his consent; it was too bad, even for France, and caused a general horror. The duke's heir hastened to make a treaty with King Henry, and the French Queen engaged that her husband should consent to it, whatever it was. Henry made peace, on condition of receiving the Princess Catherine in marriage, and being made Regent of France during the rest of the King's life-time, and succeeding to the French crown at his death. He was soon married to the beautiful Princess, and took her proudly home to England, where she was crowned with great honor and glory.

This peace was called the Perpetual Peace; we shall soon see how long it lasted. It gave great satisfaction to the French people, although they were so poor and miserable, that, at the time of the celebration of the Royal marriage, numbers of them were dying with starvation, on the dunghills in the streets of Paris. There was some resistance, on the part of the Dauphin in some few parts of France, but King Henry beat it all down.

And now, with his great possessions in France secured, and his beautiful wife to cheer him, and a son born to give him greater happiness, all appeared bright before him.   But, in the fulness of his triumph and the height of his power, Death came upon him, and his day was done.   When he fell ill at Vincennes, and found that he could not recover, he was very calm and quiet, and spoke serenely to those who wept around his bed.   His wife and child, he said, he left to the loving care of his brother the Duke of Bedford, and his other faithful nobles.   He gave them his advice that England should establish a friendship with the new Duke of Burgundy, and offer him the regency of France ; that it should not set free the royal princes who had been taken at Agincourt; and that, whatever quarrel might arise with France, England should never make peace without holding Normandy.   Then, he laid down his head, and asked the attendant priests to chant the penitential psalms.   Amid which solemn sounds, on the thirty-first of August, one thousand four hundred and twenty-two, in only the thirty-fourth year of his age and the tenth of his reign, King Henry the Fifth passed away.

Slowly and mournfully they carried his embalmed body in a procession of great state to Paris, and thence

to Rouen where his Queen was : from whom the sad
intelligence of his death was concealed until he had
been dead some days. Thence, lying on a bed of
crimson and gold, with a golden crown upon the head,
and a golden ball and sceptre lying in the nerveless
hands, they carried it to Calais, with such a great
retinue as seemed to dye the road black. The
King of Scotland acted as chief mourner, all the
Royal Household followed, the knights wore black
armour and black plumes of feathers, crowds of men
bore torches, making the night as light as day ; and
the widowed Princess followed last of all. At Calais
there was a fleet of ships to bring the funeral host to
Dover, and so, by way of London Bridge, where the
service for the dead was chanted as it passed along, they
brought the body to Westminster Abbey, and there
buried it with great respect.

CHAPTER XXII.

ENGLAND UNDER HENRY THE SIXTH.

Part the First.

It had been the wish of the late King, that while his
infant son King Henry the Sixth, at this time only
nine months old, was under age, the Duke of Gloucester
should be appointed Regent.   The English Parliament,
however, preferred to appoint a Council of Regency,
with the Duke of Bedford at its head: to be represented, in his absence only, by the Duke of Gloucester.
The Parliament would seem to have been wise in this,
for Gloucester soon showed himself to be ambitious
and troublesome, and, in the gratification of his own
personal schemes, gave dangerous offence to the Duke
of Burgundy, which was with difficulty adjusted.

As that duke declined the Regency of France, it was
bestowed by the poor French King upon the Duke of
Bedford.   But, the French King dying within two

months, the Dauphin instantly asserted his claim to
the French throne, and was actually crowned under
the title of CHARLES THE SEVENTH. The Duke of
Bedford, to be a match for him, entered into a friendly
league with the Dukes of Burgundy and Brittany, and
gave them his two sisters in marriage. War with
France was immediately renewed, and the Perpetual
Peace came to an untimely end.

In the first campaign, the English, aided by this
alliance, were speedily successful. As Scotland, however, had sent the French five thousand men, and
might send more, or attack the North of England while
England was busy with France, it was considered that
it would be a good thing to offer the Scottish King,
James, who had been so long imprisoned, his liberty,
on his paying forty thousand pounds for his board and
lodging during nineteen years, and engaging to forbid
his subjects from serving under the flag of France.
It is pleasant to know, not only that the amiable captive
at last regained his freedom upon these terms, but, that
he married a noble English lady with whom he had
been long in love, and became an excellent King. I
am afraid we have met with some Kings in this history,
and shall meet with some more, who would have been
very much the better, and would have left the world

much happier, if they had been imprisoned nineteen years too.

In the second campaign, the English gained a considerable victory at Verneuil, in a battle which was chiefly remarkable, otherwise, for their resorting to the odd expedient of tying their baggage-horses together by the heads and tails, and jumbling them up with the baggage, so as to convert them into a sort of live fortification—which was found useful to the troops, but which I should think was not agreeable to the horses. For three years afterwards very little was done, owing to both sides being too poor for war, which is a very expensive entertainment; but, a council was then held in Paris, in which it was decided to lay siege to the town of Orleans, which was a place of great importance to the Dauphin's cause. An English army of ten thousand men was dispatched on this service, under the command of the Earl of Salisbury, a general of fame. He being unfortunately killed early in the siege, the Earl of Suffolk took his place; under whom (reinforced by SIR JOHN FALSTAFF, who brought up four hundred waggons laden with salt herrings and other provisions for the troops, and, beating off the French who tried to intercept him, came victorious out of a hot skirmish, which was afterwards called in jest the Battle of the Herrings), the town of Orleans was so completely hemmed in, that the besieged proposed to yield it up to their countryman the Duke of Burgundy. The English general, however, replied that his English men had won it, so far, by their blood and valor, and that his English men must have it. There seemed to be no hope for the town, or for the Dauphin, who was so dismayed that he even thought of flying to Scotland or to Spain—when a peasant girl rose up and changed the whole state of affairs.

The story of this peasant girl I have now to tell.

PART THE SECOND.

THE STORY OF JOAN OF ARC.

In a remote village among some wild hills in the province of Lorraine, there lived a countryman whose name was JACQUES D'ARC. He had a daughter, JOAN OF ARC, who was at this time in her twentieth year. She had been a solitary girl from her childhood; she had often tended sheep and cattle for whole days where no human figure was seen or human voice heard; and she had often knelt, for hours together, in the gloomy empty little village chapel, looking up at the altar and at the dim lamp burning before it, until she fancied that she saw shadowy figures standing there, and even that she heard them speak to her. The people in that part of France were very ignorant and superstitious, and they had many ghostly tales to tell about what they dreamed, and what they saw among the lonely hills when the clouds and the mists were resting on them. So, they easily believed that Joan saw strange sights, and they whispered among themselves that angels and spirits talked to her.

At last, Joan told her father that she had one day been surprised by a great unearthly light, and had afterwards heard a solemn voice, which said it was Saint Michael's voice, telling her that she was to go and help the Dauphin. Soon after this (she said), Saint Catherine and Saint Margaret had appeared to her, with sparkling crowns upon their heads, and had encouraged her to be virtuous and resolute. These visions had returned sometimes; but the Voices very often; and the voices always said, " Joan, thou art appointed by Heaven to go and help the Dauphin !" She almost always heard them while the chapel bells were ringing.

There is no doubt, now, that Joan believed she saw and heard these things. It is very well known that such delusions are a disease which is not by any means uncommon. It is probable enough that there were figures of Saint Michael, and Saint Catherine, and Saint Margaret, in the little chapel (where they would be very likely to have shining crowns upon their heads), and that they first gave Joan the idea of those three personages. She had long been a moping, fanciful girl, and, though she was a very good girl, I dare say she was a little vain, and wishful for notoriety.

Her father, something wiser than his neighbours, said, "I tell thee, Joan, it is thy fancy. Thou hadst better have a kind husband to take care of thee, girl, and work to employ thy mind!" But Joan told him in reply, that she had taken a vow never to have a husband, and that she must go as Heaven directed her, to help the Dauphin.

It happened, unfortunately for her father's persuasions, and most unfortunately for the poor girl, too, that a party of the Dauphin's enemies found their way into the village while Joan's disorder was at this point, and burnt the chapel, and drove out the inhabitants. The cruelties she saw committed, touched Joan's heart and made her worse. She said that the voices and the figures were now continually with her; that they told her she was the girl who, according to an old prophecy, was to deliver France; that she must go and help the Dauphin, and must remain with him until he should be crowned at Rheims: and that she must travel a long way to a certain lord named BAUDRICOURT, who could and would, bring her into the Dauphin's presence.

As her father still said, "I tell thee, Joan, it is thy fancy," she set off to find out this lord, accompanied by an uncle, a poor village wheelwright and cart-maker, who believed in the reality of her visions. They travelled a long way and went on and on, over a rough country, full of the Duke of Burgundy's men, and of all kinds of robbers and marauders, until they came to where this lord was.

When his servants told him that there was a poor peasant girl named Joan of Arc, accompanied by nobody but an old village wheelwright and cart-maker, who wished to see him because she was commanded to help the Dauphin and save France, Baudricourt burst out a-laughing, and bade them send the girl away. But, he soon heard so much about her lingering in the town, and praying in the churches, and seeing visions, and doing harm to no one, that he sent for her, and questioned her. As she said the same things after she had been well sprinkled with holy water as she had said before the sprinkling, Baudricourt began to think there might be something in it. At all events, he thought it worth while to send her on to the town of Chinon, where the Dauphin was. So, he bought her a horse, and a sword, and gave her two squires to conduct her. As the Voices had told Joan that she was to wear a man's dress, now, she put one on, and girded her sword to her side, and bound spurs to her heels, and mounted her horse and rode away with her two squires. As to her uncle the wheelwright, he stood staring at his niece in wonder until she was out of sight—as well he might—and then went home again. The best place, too.

Joan and her two squires rode on and on, until they came to Chinon, where she was, after some doubt, admitted into the Dauphin's presence. Picking him out immediately from all his court, she told him that she came commanded by Heaven to subdue his enemies and conduct him to his coronation at Rheims. She also told him (or he pretended so afterwards to make the greater impression upon his soldiers) a number of his secrets known only to himself, and, furthermore, she said there was an old, old sword in the cathedral of Saint Catherine at Fierbois, marked with five old crosses on the blade, which Saint Catherine had ordered her to wear.

Now, nobody knew anything about this old, old sword, but when the cathedral came to be examined—which was immediately done—there, sure enough, the sword was found! The Dauphin then required a number of grave priests and bishops to give him their opinion whether the girl derived her power from good spirits or from evil spirits, which they held prodigiously long debates about, in the course of which several learned men fell fast asleep and snored loudly. At

last, when one gruff old gentleman had said to Joan,
"What language do your Voices speak?" and when
Joan had replied to the gruff old gentleman "A
pleasanter language than yours," they agreed that it
was all correct, and that Joan of Arc was inspired from
Heaven. This wonderful circumstance put new heart
into the Dauphin's soldiers when they heard of it,
and dispirited the English army, who took Joan for
a witch.

So Joan mounted horse again, and again rode on
and on, until she came to Orleans. But she rode now,
as never peasant girl had ridden yet. She rode upon
a white war-horse, in a suit of glittering armour; with
the old, old sword from the cathedral, newly burnished,
in her belt; with a white flag carried before her, upon
which were a picture of God, and the words JESUS
MARIA. In this splendid state, at the head of a great
body of troops escorting provisions of all kinds for the
starving inhabitants of Orleans, she appeared before that
beleaguered city.

When the people on the walls beheld her, they cried
out " The Maid is come! The Maid of the Prophecy
is come to deliver us!" And this, and the sight of
the Maid fighting at the head of their men, made the
French so bold, and made the English so fearful, that

the English line of forts were soon broken, the troops and provisions were got into the town, and Orleans was saved.

Joan, henceforth called THE MAID OF ORLEANS, remained within the walls for a few days, and caused letters to be thrown over, ordering Lord Suffolk and his Englishmen to depart from before the town according to the will of Heaven. As the English general very positively declined to believe that Joan knew anything about the will of Heaven (which did not mend the matter with his soldiers, for they stupidly said if she were not inspired she was a witch, and it was of no use to fight against a witch), she mounted her white war-horse again, and ordered her white banner to advance.

The besiegers held the bridge, and some strong towers upon the bridge ; and here the Maid of Orleans attacked them. The fight was fourteen hours long. She planted a scaling ladder with her own hands, and mounted a tower wall, but was struck by an English arrow in the neck, and fell into the trench. She was carried away and the arrow was taken out, during which operation she screamed and cried with the pain, as any other girl might have done ; but presently she said that the Voices were speaking to her and soothing her to rest. After a while, she got up, and was again foremost in the fight. When the English who had seen her fall and supposed her to be dead, saw this, they were troubled with the strangest fears, and some of them cried out that they beheld St. Michael on a white horse (probably Joan herself) fighting for the French. They lost the bridge, and lost the towers, and next day set their chain of forts on fire, and left the place.

But as Lord Suffolk himself retired no farther than the town of Jargeau, which was only a few miles off, the Maid of Orleans besieged him there, and he was taken prisoner. As the white banner scaled the wall, she was struck upon the head with a stone, and was again tumbled down into the ditch; but, she only cried all the more, as she lay there, " On, on, my country-men! And fear nothing, for the Lord hath delivered them into our hands!" After this new success of the Maid's, several other fortresses and places which had previously held out against the Dauphin were delivered up without a battle; and at Patay she defeated the remainder of the English army, and set up her victorious white banner on a field where twelve hundred Englishmen lay dead.

She now urged the Dauphin (who always kept out of the way when there was any fighting) to proceed to Rheims, as the first part of her mission was accomplished; and to complete the whole by being crowned there. The Dauphin was in no particular hurry to do this, as Rheims was a long way off, and the English and the Duke of Burgundy were still strong in the country through which the road lay. However, they set forth, with ten thousand men, and again the Maid of Orleans rode on and on, upon her white war-horse, and in her shining armour. Whenever they came to a town which yielded readily, the soldiers believed in her; but, whenever they came to a town which gave them any trouble, they began to murmur that she was an impostor. The latter was particularly the case at Troyes, which finally yielded, however, through the persuasion of one Richard, a friar of the place. Friar Richard was in the old doubt about the Maid of Orleans, until he had sprinkled her well with holy water, and had also well sprinkled the threshold of the gate by which she came into the city. Finding that it made no change in her or the gate, he said, as the other grave old gentlemen had said, that it was all right, and became her great ally.

So, at last, by dint of riding on and on, the Maid of Orleans, and the Dauphin, and the ten thousand some-

times believing and sometimes unbelieving men, came
to Rheims.   And in the great cathedral of Rheims, the
Dauphin actually was crowned Charles the Seventh in
a great assembly of the people.   Then, the Maid, who
with her white banner stood beside the King in that
hour of his triumph, kneeled down upon the pavement
at his feet, and said, with tears, that what she had been
inspired to do, was done, and that the only recompense
she asked for, was, that she should now have leave to go
back to her distant home, and her sturdily incredulous
father, and her first simple. escort the village wheelwright and cart-maker.   But the King said "No!"
and made her and her family as noble as a King could,
and settled upon her the income of a Count.

Ah! happy had it been for the Maid of Orleans, if
she had resumed her rustic dress that day, and had
gone home to the little chapel and the wild hills, and
had forgotten all these things, and had been a good
man's wife, and had heard no stranger voices than the
voices of little children!

It was not to be, and she continued helping the
King (she did a world for him, in alliance with Friar
Richard), and trying to improve the lives of the coarse
soldiers, and leading a religious, an unselfish, and a
modest life, herself, beyond any doubt.   Still, many

times she prayed the King to let her go home ; and
once she even took off her bright armour and hung it
up in a church, meaning never to wear it more. But,
the King always won her back again—while she was of
any use to him—and so she went on and on and on,
to her doom.

When the Duke of Bedford, who was a very able
man, began to be active for England, and, by bringing
the war back into France and by holding the Duke of
Burgundy to his faith, to distress and disturb Charles
very much, Charles sometimes asked the Maid of
Orleans what the Voices said about it ? But, the
Voices had become (very like ordinary voices in per-
plexed times,) contradictory and confused, so that now
they said one thing, and now said another, and the Maid
lost credit every day.   Charles marched on Paris, which
was opposed to him, and attacked the suburb of Saint
Honoré.   In this fight, being again struck down into
the ditch, she was abandoned by the whole army.   She
lay unaided among a heap of dead, and crawled out
how she could.   Then, some of her believers went over
to an opposition Maid, Catherine of La Rochelle, who
said she was inspired to tell where there were treasures
of buried money—though she never did—and then Joan
accidentally broke the old, old sword, and others said

that her power was broken with it. Finally, at the
siege of Compiègne, held by the Duke of Burgundy,
where she did valiant service, she was basely left alone
in a retreat, though facing about and fighting to the
last; and an archer pulled her off her horse.

O the uproar that was made, and the thanksgivings
that were sung, about the capture of this one poor
country-girl! O the way in which she was demanded
to be tried for sorcery and heresy, and anything else
you like, by the Inquisitor-General of France, and by
this great man, and by that great man, until it is
wearisome to think of! She was bought at last by the
Bishop of Beauvais for ten thousand francs, and was
shut up in her narrow prison: plain Joan of Arc again,
and Maid of Orleans no more.

I should never have done if I were to tell you how
they had Joan out to examine her, and cross-examine
her, and re-examine her, and worry her into saying
anything and everything; and how all sorts of scholars
and doctors bestowed their utmost tediousness upon
her. Sixteen times she was brought out and shut up
again, and worried, and entrapped, and argued with,
until she was heart-sick of the dreary business. On
the last occasion of this kind she was brought into a
burial-place at Rouen, dismally decorated with a scaf-

fold, and a stake and faggots, and the executioner, and
a pulpit with a friar therein, and an awful sermon ready.
It is very affecting to know that even at that pass the
poor girl honored the mean vermin of a King, who had
so used her for his purposes and so abandoned her;
and, that while she had been regardless of reproaches
heaped upon herself, she spoke out courageously for
him.

It was natural in one so young to hold to life. To
save her life, she signed a declaration prepared for her
—signed it with a cross, for she couldn't write—that
all her visions and Voices had come from the Devil.
Upon her recanting the past, and protesting that she
would never wear a man's dress in future, she was condemned to imprisonment for life, "on the bread of
sorrow and the water of affliction."

But, on the bread of sorrow and the water of affliction, the visions and the Voices soon returned. It was
quite natural that they should do so, for that kind of
disease is much aggravated by fasting, loneliness, and
anxiety of mind. It was not only got out of Joan that
she considered herself inspired again, but, she was
taken in a man's dress, which had been left—to entrap
her—in her prison, and which she put on, in her soli-
tude; perhaps, in remembrance of her past glories;

perhaps, because the imaginary Voices told her. For this relapse into the sorcery and heresy and anything else you like, she was sentenced to be burnt to death. And, in the market-place of Rouen, in the hideous dress which the monks had invented for such spectacles; with priests and bishops sitting in a gallery looking on, though some had the Christian grace to go away, unable to endure the infamous scene ; this shrieking girl—last seen amidst the smoke and fire, holding a crucifix between her hands; last heard, calling upon Christ—was burnt to ashes. They threw her ashes into the river Seine ; but, they will rise against her murderers on the last day.

From the moment of her capture, neither the French King nor one single man in all his court raised a finger to save her. It is no defence of them that they may have never really believed in her, or that they may have won her victories by their skill and bravery. The more they pretended to believe in her, the more they had caused her to believe in herself; and she had ever been true to them, ever brave, ever nobly devoted. But, it is no wonder, that they, who were in all things false to themselves, false to one another, false to their country, false to Heaven, and false to Earth, should be monsters of ingratitude and treachery to a helpless peasant girl.

In the picturesque old town of Rouen, where weeds

and grass grow high on the cathedral towers, and the venerable Norman streets are still warm in the blessed sunlight though the monkish fires that once gleamed horribly upon them have long grown cold, there is a statue of Joan of Arc, in the scene of her last agony, the square to which she has given its present name. I know some statues of modern times—even in the World's metropolis, I think—which commemorate less constancy, less earnestness, smaller claims upon the world's attention, and much greater impostors.

PART THE THIRD.

BAD deeds seldom prosper, happily for mankind; and
the English cause gained no advantage from the cruel
death of Joan of Arc. For a long time, the war went
heavily on. The Duke of Bedford died; the alliance
with the Duke of Burgundy was broken; and Lord
Talbot became a great general on the English side in
France. But, two of the consequences of wars are,
Famine—because the people cannot peacefully cultivate
the ground—and Pestilence, which comes of want,
misery, and suffering. Both these horrors broke
out in both countries, and lasted for two wretched
years. Then, the war went on again, and came by
slow degrees to be so badly conducted by the English
government, that, within twenty years from the
execution of the Maid of Orleans, of all the great
French conquests, the town of Calais alone remained
in English hands.

While these victories and defeats were taking place in the course of time, many strange things happened at home. The young King, as he grew up, proved to be very unlike his great father, and showed himself a miserable puny creature. There was no harm in him —he had a great aversion to shedding blood: which was something—but, he was a weak, silly, helpless young man, and a mere shuttlecock to the great lordly battledores about the Court.

Of these battledores, Cardinal Beaufort a relation of the King, and the Duke of Gloucester, were at first the most powerful. The Duke of Gloucester had a wife, who was nonsensically accused of practising witchcraft to cause the King's death and lead to her husband's coming to the throne, he being the next heir. She was charged with having, by the help of a ridiculous old woman named Margery (who was called a witch), made a little waxen doll in the King's likeness, and put it before a slow fire that it might gradually melt away. It was supposed, in such cases, that the death of the person whom the doll was made to represent, was sure to happen. Whether the duchess was as ignorant as the rest of them, and really did make such a doll with such an intention, I don't know; but, you and I know very well that she might have made a thousand dolls, if she had been stupid enough, and might have melted them all, without hurting the King or anybody else. However, she was tried for it, and so was old Margery, and so was one of the duke's chaplains, who was charged with having assisted them. Both he and Margery were put to death, and the duchess, after being taken, on foot and bearing a lighted candle, three times round the City as a penance, was imprisoned for life. The duke, himself, took all this pretty quietly, and made as little stir about the matter as if he were rather glad to be rid of the duchess.

But, he was not destined to keep himself out of trouble long. The royal shuttlecock being three-and-twenty, the battledores were very anxious to get him married. The Duke of Gloucester wanted him to marry a daughter of the Count of Armagnac; but, the Cardinal and the Earl of Suffolk were all for MARGARET, the daughter of the King of Sicily, who they knew was a resolute ambitious woman and would govern the King as she chose. To make friends with this lady, the Earl of Suffolk, who went over to arrange the match, consented to accept her for the King's wife without any fortune, and even to give up the two most valuable possessions England then had in France.

So, the marriage was arranged, on terms very advantageous to the lady; and Lord Suffolk brought her to England, and she was married at Westminster. On what pretence this queen and her party charged the Duke of Gloucester with high treason within a couple of years, it is impossible to make out, the matter is so confused; but, they pretended that the King's life was in danger, and they took the duke prisoner. A fortnight afterwards, he was found dead in bed (they said), and his body was shown to the people, and Lord Suffolk came in for the best part of his estates. You know by this time how strangely liable state prisoners were to sudden death.

If Cardinal Beaufort had any hand in this matter, it did him no good, for he died within six weeks; thinking it very hard and curious—at eighty years old! —that he could not live to be Pope.

This was the time when England had completed her loss of all her great French conquests. The people charged the loss principally upon the Earl of Suffolk, now a duke, who had made those easy terms about the Royal marriage, and who, they believed, had even been bought by France. So he was impeached as a traitor, on a great number of charges, but chiefly on accusations of having aided the French King, and of designing to make his own son King of England. The Commons and the people being violent against him, the King was made (by his friends) to interpose to save him, by banishing him for five years, and proroguing the Parliament. The duke had much ado to escape from a London mob, two thousand strong, who lay in wait for him in St. Giles's fields; but, he got down to his own estates in Suffolk, and sailed away from Ipswich. Sailing across the Channel, he sent into Calais to know if he might land there; but, they kept his boat and men in the harbour, until an English ship, carrying a hundred and fifty men and called the Nicholas of the Tower, came alongside his little vessel, and ordered him on board. "Welcome, traitor, as men say," was the captain's grim and not very respectful salutation. He was kept on board, a prisoner, for eight-and-forty hours, and then a small boat appeared rowing towards the ship. As this boat came nearer, it was seen to have in it a block, a rusty sword, and an executioner in a black mask. The duke was handed down into it, and there his head was cut off with six strokes of the rusty sword. Then, the little boat rowed away to Dover beach, where the body was cast out, and left until the duchess claimed it. By whom, high in authority, this murder was committed, has never appeared. No one was ever punished for it.

There now arose in Kent an Irishman, who gave himself the name of Mortimer, but whose real name was JACK CADE. Jack, in imitation of Wat Tyler, though he was a very different and inferior sort of man, addressed the Kentish men upon their wrongs, occasioned by the bad government of England, among so many battledores and such a poor shuttlecock; and the Kentish men rose up to the number of twenty thousand. Their place of assembly was Blackheath, where, headed by Jack, they put forth two papers, which they called " The Complaint of the Commons of Kent," and " The Requests of the Captain of the Great Assembly in Kent." They then retired to Sevenoaks. The royal army coming up with them here, they beat it and killed their general. Then, Jack dressed himself in the dead general's armour, and led his men to London.

Jack passed into the City from Southwark, over the bridge, and entered it in triumph, giving the strictest orders to his men not to plunder. Having made a show of his forces there, while the citizens looked on quietly, he went back into Southwark in good order, and passed the night. Next day, he came back

again, having got hold in the meantime of Lord
Say, an unpopular nobleman. Says Jack to the Lord
Mayor and judges: "Will you be so good as to
make a tribunal in Guildhall, and try me this nobleman?" The court being hastily made, he was found
guilty, and Jack and his men cut his head off on
Cornhill. They also cut off the head of his son-in-
law, and then went back in good order to Southwark
again.

But, although the citizens could bear the beheading
of an unpopular lord, they could not bear to have their
houses pillaged. And it did so happen that Jack, after
dinner — perhaps he had drunk a little too much —
began to plunder the house where he lodged; upon
which, of course, his men began to imitate him.
Wherefore, the Londoners took counsel with Lord
Scales, who had a thousand soldiers in the Tower;
and defended London Bridge, and kept Jack and his
people out. This advantage gained, it was resolved by
divers great men to divide Jack's army in the old way,
by making a great many promises on behalf of the
state, that were never intended to be performed. This
did divide them; some of Jack's men saying that they
ought to take the conditions which were offered, and
others saying that they ought not, for they were only a

snare; some going home at once; others staying where they were; and all doubting and quarrelling among themselves.

Jack, who was in two minds about fighting or accepting a pardon, and who indeed did both, saw at last that there was nothing to expect from his men, and that it was very likely some of them would deliver him up and get a reward of a thousand marks, which was offered for his apprehension. So, after they had travelled and quarrelled all the way from Southwark to Blackheath, and from Blackheath to Rochester, he mounted a good horse and galloped away into Sussex. But, there galloped after him, on a better horse, one Alexander Iden, who came up with him, had a hard fight with him, and killed him. Jack's head was set aloft on London Bridge, with the face looking towards Blackheath, where he had raised his flag; and Alexander Iden got the thousand marks.

It is supposed by some, that the Duke of York, who had been removed from a high post abroad through the Queen's influence, and sent out of the way, to govern Ireland, was at the bottom of this rising of Jack and his men, because he wanted to trouble the Government. He claimed (though not yet publicly) to have a better right to the throne than Henry of

Lancaster, as one of the family of the Earl of March, whom Henry the Fourth had set aside. Touching this claim, which, being through female relationship, was not according to the usual descent, it is enough to say that Henry the Fourth was the free choice of the people and the Parliament, and that his family had now reigned undisputed for sixty years. The memory of Henry the Fifth was so famous, and the English people loved it so much, that the Duke of York's claim would, perhaps, never have been thought of (it would have been so hopeless) but for the unfortunate circumstance of the present King's being by this time quite an idiot, and the country very badly governed. These two circumstances gave the Duke of York a power he could not otherwise have had.

Whether the Duke knew anything of Jack Cade, or not, he came over from Ireland while Jack's head was on London Bridge; being secretly advised that the Queen was setting up his enemy, the Duke of Somerset, against him. He went to Westminster, at the head of four thousand men, and on his knees before the King, represented to him the bad state of the country, and petitioned him to summon a Parliament to consider it. This the King promised. When the Parliament was summoned, the Duke of York accused the Duke of

Somerset, and the Duke of Somerset accused the Duke of York; and, both in and out of Parliament, the followers of each party were full of violence and hatred towards the other. At length the Duke of York put himself at the head of a large force of his tenants, and, in arms, demanded the reformation of the Government. Being shut out of London, he encamped at Dartford, and the royal army encamped at Blackheath. According as either side triumphed, the Duke of York was arrested, or the Duke of Somerset was arrested. The trouble ended, for the moment, in the Duke of York renewing his oath of allegiance, and going in peace to one of his own castles.

Half a year afterwards the Queen gave birth to a son, who was very ill received by the people, and not believed to be the son of the King. It shows the Duke of York to have been a moderate man, unwilling to involve England in new troubles, that he did not take advantage of the general discontent at this time, but really acted for the public good. He was made a member of the cabinet, and the King being now so much worse that he could not be carried about and shown to the people with any decency, the duke was made Lord Protector of the kingdom, until he should recover, or the Prince should come of age. At the

same time the Duke of Somerset was committed to the
Tower. So, now the Duke of Somerset was down, and
the Duke of York was up. By the end of the year,
however, the King recovered his memory and some
spark of sense; upon which the Queen used her power
—which recovered with him—to get the Protector disgraced, and her favorite released. So now the Duke
of York was down, and the Duke of Somerset was up.

These ducal ups and downs gradually separated the
whole nation into the two parties of York and Lancaster, and led to those terrible civil wars long known
as the Wars of the Red and White Roses, because the
red rose was the badge of the House of Lancaster,
and the white rose was the badge of the House of
York.

The Duke of York, joined by some other powerful
noblemen of the White Rose party, and leading a small
army, met the King with another small army at St.
Alban's, and demanded that the Duke of Somerset
should be given up. The poor King, being made to
say in answer that he would sooner die, was instantly
attacked. The Duke of Somerset was killed, and the
King himself was wounded in the neck, and took
refuge in the house of a poor tanner. Whereupon, the
Duke of York went to him, led him with great sub-

mission to the Abbey, and said he was very sorry for what had happened. Having now the King in his possession, he got a Parliament summoned and himself once more made Protector, but, only for a few months; for, on the King getting a little better again, the Queen and her party got him into their possession, and disgraced the Duke once more. So, now the Duke of York was down again.

Some of the best men in power, seeing the danger of these constant changes, tried even then to prevent the Red and White Rose Wars. They brought about a great council in London between the two parties. The White Roses assembled in Blackfriars, the Red Roses in Whitefriars; and some good priests communicated between them, and made the proceedings known at evening to the King and the judges. They ended in a peaceful agreement that there should be no more quarrelling; and there was a great royal procession to St. Paul's, in which the Queen walked arm-in-arm with her old enemy, the Duke of York, to show the people how comfortable they all were. This state of peace lasted half a year, when a dispute between the Earl of Warwick (one of the Duke's powerful friends) and some of the King's servants at Court, led to an attack upon that Earl—who was a White Rose—and to a sudden breaking out of all the old animosities.   So, here were greater ups and downs than ever.

There were even greater ups and downs than these, soon after.   After various battles, the Duke of York fled to Ireland, and his son the Earl of March to Calais, with their friends the Earls of Salisbury and Warwick; and a Parliament was held declaring them all traitors.   Little the worse for this, the Earl of Warwick presently came back, landed in Kent, was joined by the Archbishop of Canterbury and other powerful noblemen and gentlemen, engaged the King's forces at Northampton, signally defeated them, and took the King himself prisoner, who was found in his tent. Warwick would have been glad, I dare say, to have taken the Queen and Prince too, but they escaped into Wales and thence into Scotland.

The King was carried by the victorious force straight to London, and made to call a new Parliament, which immediately declared that the Duke of York and those other noblemen were not traitors, but excellent subjects. Then, back comes the Duke from Ireland at the head of five hundred horsemen, rides from London to Westminster, and enters the House of Lords.   There, he laid his hand upon the cloth of gold which covered the empty throne, as if he had half a mind to sit down in it—but he did not. On the Archbishop of Canterbury asking him if he would visit the King, who was in the palace close by, he replied "I know no one in this country, my lord, who ought not to visit *me*." None of the lords present, spoke a single word ; so, the duke went out as he had come in, established himself royally in the King's palace, and, six days afterwards, sent in to the Lords a formal statement of his claim to the throne. The lords went to the King on this momentous subject, and after a great deal of discussion, in which the judges and the other law officers were afraid to give an opinion on either side, the question was compromised. It was agreed that the present King should retain the crown for his life, and that it should then pass to the Duke of York and his heirs.

But, the resolute Queen, determined on asserting her son's rights, would hear of no such thing. She came from Scotland to the north of England, where several powerful lords armed in her cause. The Duke of York, for his part, set off with some five thousand men, a little time before Christmas Day, one thousand four hundred and sixty, to give her battle. He lodged at Sandal Castle, near Wakefield, and the Red Roses defied him to come out on Wakefield Green, and fight them then and there. His generals said, he had best wait until his gallant son, the Earl of March, came up with his power; but, he was determined to accept the challenge. He did so, in an evil hour. He was hotly pressed on all sides, two thousand of his men lay dead on Wakefield Green, and he himself was taken prisoner. They set him down in mock state on an ant-hill, and twisted grass about his head, and pretended to pay court to him on their knees, saying, " O King, without a kingdom, and Prince without a people, we hope your gracious Majesty is very well and happy!" They did worse than this; they cut his head off, and handed it on a pole to the Queen, who laughed with delight when she saw it (you recollect their walking so religiously and comfortably to St. Paul's !), and had it fixed, with a paper crown upon its head, on the walls of York. The Earl of Salisbury lost his head, too; and the Duke of York's second son, a handsome boy who was flying with his tutor over Wakefield Bridge, was stabbed in the heart by a murderous lord — Lord Clifford by name — whose father had been killed by the White Roses in the fight at St. Alban's. There was awful sacrifice of life in this battle, for no quarter was given, and the Queen was wild for revenge. When men unnaturally fight against their own countrymen, they are always observed to be more unnaturally cruel and filled with rage than they are against any other enemy.

But, Lord Clifford had stabbed the second son of the Duke of York—not the first. The eldest son, Edward Earl of March, was at Gloucester; and, vowing vengeance for the death of his father, his brother, and their faithful friends, he began to march against the Queen. He had to turn and fight a great body of Welsh and Irish first, who worried his advance. These he defeated in a great fight at Mortimer's Cross, near Hereford, where he beheaded a number of the Red Roses taken in battle, in retaliation for the beheading of the White Roses at Wakefield. The Queen had the next turn of beheading. Having moved towards London, and falling in, between St. Alban's and Barnet, with the Earl of Warwick and the Duke of Norfolk, White Roses both, who were there with an army to oppose her, and had got the King with them; she defeated them with great loss, and struck off the heads of two prisoners of note, who were in the King's tent with him, and to whom the King had promised his protection. Her triumph, however, was very short. She had no treasure, and her army subsisted by plunder. This caused them to be hated and dreaded by the people, and particularly by the

London people, who were wealthy. As soon as the Londoners heard that Edward, Earl of March, united with the Earl of Warwick, was advancing towards the city, they refused to send the Queen supplies, and made a great rejoicing.

The Queen and her men retreated with all speed, and Edward and Warwick came on, greeted with loud acclamations on every side. The courage, beauty, and virtues of young Edward could not be sufficiently praised by the whole people. He rode into London like a conqueror, and met with an enthusiastic welcome. A few days afterwards, Lord Falconbridge and the Bishop of Exeter assembled the citizens in St. John's Field, Clerkenwell, and asked them if they would have Henry of Lancaster for their King? To this they all roared, "No, no, no!" and "King Edward! King Edward!" Then, said those noblemen, would they love and serve young Edward? To this they all cried, "Yes, yes!" and threw up their caps and clapped their hands, and cheered tremendously.

Therefore, it was declared that by joining the Queen and not protecting those two prisoners of note, Henry of Lancaster had forfeited the crown; and Edward of York was proclaimed King. He made a great speech to the applauding people at Westminster, and sat down as sovereign of England on that throne, on the golden covering of which his father—worthy of a better fate than the bloody axe which cut the thread of so many lives in England, through so many years—had laid his hand.

CHAPTER XXIII.

ENGLAND UNDER EDWARD THE FOURTH.

KING EDWARD THE FOURTH was not quite twenty-one years of age when he took that unquiet seat upon the throne of England. The Lancaster party, the Red Roses, were then assembling in great numbers near York, and it was necessary to give them battle instantly. But, the stout Earl of Warwick leading for the young King, and the young King himself closely following him, and the English people crowding to the Royal standard, the White and the Red Roses met, on a wild March day when the snow was falling heavily, at Towton; and there such a furious battle raged between them, that the total loss amounted to forty thousand men — all Englishmen, fighting, upon English ground, against one another. The young King gained the day, took down the heads of his father and brother from the walls of York, and put up the heads of some of the most famous noblemen engaged in the battle on the other side. Then, he went to London and was crowned with great splendour.

A new Parliament met. No fewer than one hundred and fifty of the principal noblemen and gentlemen on the Lancaster side were declared traitors, and the King —who had very little humanity, though he was handsome in person and agreeable in manners—resolved to do all he could, to pluck up the Red Rose root and branch.

Queen Margaret, however, was still active for her young son. She obtained help from Scotland and from Normandy, and took several important English castles. But, Warwick soon retook them; the Queen lost all her treasure on board ship in a great storm; and both she and her son suffered great misfortunes. Once, in the winter weather, as they were riding through a forest, they were attacked and plundered by a party of robbers; and, when they had escaped from these men and were passing alone and on foot through a thick dark part of the wood, they came, all at once, upon another robber. So the Queen, with a stout heart, took the little Prince by the hand, and going straight up to that robber, said to him, " My friend, this is the young son of your lawful King! I confide him to your care." The robber was surprised, but took the boy in his arms, and faithfully restored him and his mother to their friends. In the end, the Queen's soldiers being beaten and dispersed, she went abroad again, and kept quiet for the present.

Now, all this time, the deposed King Henry was concealed by a Welsh knight, who kept him close in his castle. But, next year, the Lancaster party recovering their spirits, raised a large body of men, and called him out of his retirement, to put him at their head. They were joined by some powerful noblemen who had sworn fidelity to the new King, but who were ready, as usual, to break their oaths, whenever they thought there was anything to be got by it. One of the worst things in the history of the war of the Red and White Roses, is the ease with which these noblemen, who should have set an example of honor to the people, left either side as they took slight offence, or were disappointed in their greedy expectations, and joined the other. Well! Warwick's brother soon beat the Lancastrians, and the false noblemen, being taken, were beheaded without a moment's loss of time. The deposed King had a narrow escape; three of his servants were taken, and one of them bore his cap of estate, which was set with

pearls and embroidered with two golden crowns.
However, the head to which the cap belonged, got
safely into Lancashire, and lay pretty quietly there
(the people in the secret being very true) for more than
a year. At length, an old monk gave such intelligence
as led to Henry's being taken while he was sitting at
dinner in a place called Waddington Hall. He was
immediately sent to London and met at Islington by
the Earl of Warwick, by whose directions he was
put upon a horse, with his legs tied under it, and
paraded three times round the pillory. Then, he was
carried off to the Tower, where they treated him well
enough.

The White Rose being so triumphant, the young
King abandoned himself entirely to pleasure, and led a
jovial life. But, thorns were springing up under his
bed of roses, as he soon found out. For, having been
privately married to ELIZABETH WOODVILLE, a young
widow lady, very beautiful and very captivating; and
at last resolving to make his secret known, and to
declare her his Queen; he gave some offence to the
Earl of Warwick, who was usually called the King-
Maker, because of his power and influence, and because
of his having lent such great help to placing Edward
on the throne. This offence was not lessened by the

jealousy with which the Nevil family (the Earl of Warwick's) regarded the promotion of the Woodville family.   For, the young Queen was so bent on providing for her relations, that she made her father an earl and a great officer of state; married her five sisters to young noblemen of the highest rank; and provided for her younger brother, a young man of twenty, by marrying him to an immensely rich old duchess of eighty.   The Earl of Warwick took all this pretty graciously for a man of his proud temper, until the question arose to whom the King's sister, MARGARET, should be married.   The Earl of Warwick said, "To one of the French King's sons," and was allowed to go over to the French King to make friendly proposals for that purpose, and to hold all manner of friendly interviews with him.   But, while he was so engaged, the Woodville party married the young lady to the Duke of Burgundy !   Upon this he came back in great rage and scorn, and shut himself up discontented, in his Castle of Middleham.

A reconciliation, though not a very sincere one, was patched up between the Earl of Warwick and the King, and lasted until the Earl married his daughter, against the King's wishes, to the Duke of Clarence. While the marriage was being celebrated at Calais, the

people in the north of England, where the influence of
the Nevil family was strongest, broke out into rebellion;
their complaint was, that England was oppressed and
plundered by the Woodville family, whom they demanded to have removed from power. As they were
joined by great numbers of people, and as they openly
declared that they were supported by the Earl of
Warwick, the King did not know what to do. At last,
as he wrote to the earl beseeching his aid, he and his
new son-in-law came over to England, and began to
arrange the business by shutting the King up in
Middleham Castle in the safe keeping of the Archbishop of York; so England was not only in the strange
position of having two kings at once, but they were both
prisoners at the same time.

Even as yet, however, the King-Maker was so far
true to the King, that he dispersed a new rising of the
Lancastrians, took their leader prisoner, and brought
him to the King, who ordered him to be immediately
executed. He presently allowed the King to return to
London, and there innumerable pledges of forgiveness
and friendship were exchanged between them, and
between the Nevils and the Woodvilles; the King's
eldest daughter was promised in marriage to the heir
of the Nevil family; and more friendly oaths were

sworn, and more friendly promises made, than this book would hold.

They lasted about three months. At the end of that time, the Archbishop of York made a feast for the King, the Earl of Warwick, and the Duke of Clarence, at his house, the Moor, in Hertfordshire. The King was washing his hands before supper, when some one whispered him that a body of a hundred men were lying in ambush outside the house. Whether this were true or untrue, the King took fright, mounted his horse, and rode through the dark night to Windsor Castle. Another reconciliation was patched up between him and the King-Maker, but it was a short one, and it was the last. A new rising took place in Lincoln-shire, and the King marched to repress it. Having done so, he proclaimed that both the Earl of Warwick and the Duke of Clarence were traitors, who had secretly assisted it, and who had been prepared publicly to join it, on the following day. In these dangerous circumstances they both took ship and sailed away to the French court.

And here a meeting took place between the Earl of Warwick and his old enemy, the Dowager Queen Margaret, through whom his father had had his head struck off, and to whom he had been a bitter foe. But,

now, when he said that he had done with the ungrateful
and perfidious Edward of York, and that henceforth he
devoted himself to the restoration of the House of
Lancaster, either in the person of her husband or of
her little son, she embraced him as if he had ever been
her dearest friend. She did more than that; she
married her son to his second daughter, the Lady
Anne. However agreeable this marriage was to the
two new friends, it was very disagreeable to the Duke
of Clarence, who perceived that his father-in-law, the
King-Maker, would never make *him* King, now. So,
being but a weak-minded young traitor, possessed of
very little worth or sense, he readily listened to an
artful court lady sent over for the purpose, and promised to turn traitor once more, and go over to his
brother, King Edward, when a fitting opportunity
should come.

The Earl of Warwick, knowing nothing of this, soon
redeemed his promise to the Dowager Queen Margaret,
by invading England and landing at Plymouth, where
he instantly proclaimed King Henry, and summoned
all Englishmen between the ages of sixteen and sixty,
to join his banner. Then, with his army increasing as
he marched along, he went northward, and came so
near King Edward, who was in that part of the country,

that Edward had to ride hard for it to the coast of
Norfolk, and thence to get away in such ships as he
could find, to Holland. Thereupon, the triumphant
King-Maker and his false son-in-law, the Duke of
Clarence, went to London, took the old King out of
the Tower, and walked him in a great procession to
St. Paul's cathedral with the crown upon his head.
This did not improve the temper of the Duke of
Clarence, who saw himself further off from being King
than ever ; but he kept his secret, and said nothing.
The Nevil family were restored to all their honors and
glories, and the Woodvilles and the rest were disgraced.
The King-Maker, less sanguinary than the King, shed
no blood except that of the Earl of Worcester, who had
been so cruel to the people as to have gained the title
of the Butcher. Him they caught hidden in a tree,
and him they tried and executed. No other death
stained the King-Maker's triumph.

To dispute this triumph, back came King Edward
again, next year, landing at Ravenspur, coming on to
York, causing all his men to cry "Long live King
Henry!" and swearing on the altar, without a blush,
that he came to lay no claim to the crown. Now was
the time for the Duke of Clarence, who ordered his
men to assume the White Rose, and declare for his

brother.   The Marquis of Montague, though the Earl
of Warwick's brother, also declining to fight against
King Edward, he went on successfully to London,
where the Archbishop of York let him into the City,
and where the people made great demonstrations in his
favour. For this they had four reasons. Firstly, there
were great numbers of the King's adherents hiding in
the City and ready to break out; secondly, the King
owed them a great deal of money, which they could
never hope to get if he were unsuccessful; thirdly,
there was a young prince to inherit the crown; and
fourthly, the King was gay and handsome, and more
popular than a better man might have been with the
City ladies.   After a stay of only two days with these
worthy supporters, the King marched out to Barnet
Common, to give the Earl of Warwick battle.   And
now it was to be seen, for the last time, whether the
King or the King-Maker was to carry the day.

While the battle was yet pending, the faint-hearted
Duke of Clarence began to repent, and sent over secret
messages to his father-in-law, offering his services in
mediation with the King.   But, the Earl of Warwick
disdainfully rejected them, and replied that Clarence
was false and perjured, and that he would settle the
quarrel by the sword. The battle began at four o'clock

in the morning and lasted until ten, and during the greater part of the time it was fought in a thick mist—absurdly supposed to be raised by a magician. The loss of life was very great, for the hatred was strong on both sides. The King-Maker was defeated, and the King triumphed. Both the Earl of Warwick and his brother were slain, and their bodies lay in St. Paul's, for some days, as a spectacle to the people.

Margaret's spirit was not broken even by this great blow. Within five days she was in arms again, and raised her standard in Bath, whence she set off with her army, to try and join Lord Pembroke, who had a force in Wales. But, the King, coming up with her outside the town of Tewkesbury, and ordering his brother, the DUKE OF GLOUCESTER, who was a brave soldier, to attack her men, she sustained an entire defeat, and was taken prisoner, together with her son now only eighteen years of age. The conduct of the King to this poor youth was worthy of his cruel character. He ordered him to be led into his tent. "And what," said he, " brought *you* to England?" " I came to England," replied the prisoner, with a spirit which a man of spirit might have admired in a captive, " to recover my father's kingdom, which descended to him as his right, and from him descends to me, as mine."

The King, drawing off his iron gauntlet, struck him with it in the face; and the Duke of Clarence and some other lords, who were there, drew their noble swords, and killed him.

His mother survived him, a prisoner, for five years; after her ransom by the King of France, she survived for six years more. Within three weeks of this murder, Henry died one of those convenient sudden deaths which were so common in the Tower; in plainer words, he was murdered by the King's order.

Having no particular excitement on his hands after this great defeat of the Lancaster party, and being perhaps desirous to get rid of some of his fat (for he was now getting too corpulent to be handsome), the King thought of making war on France. As he wanted more money for this purpose than the Parliament could give him, though they were usually ready enough for war, he invented a new way of raising it, by sending for the principal citizens of London, and telling them, with a grave face, that he was very much in want of cash, and would take it very kind in them if they would lend him some. It being impossible for them safely to refuse, they complied, and the monies thus forced from them were called—no doubt to the great amusement of the King and the Court—as if they were free gifts,

"Benevolences." What with grants from Parliament, and what with Benevolences, the King raised an army and passed over to Calais. As nobody wanted war, however, the French King made proposals of peace, which were accepted, and a truce was concluded for seven long years. The proceedings between the Kings of France and England on this occasion, were very friendly, very splendid, and very distrustful. They finished with a meeting between the two Kings, on a temporary bridge over the river Somme, where they embraced through two holes in a strong wooden grating like a lion's cage, and made several bows and fine speeches to one another.

It was time, now, that the Duke of Clarence should be punished for his treacheries; and Fate had his punishment in store. He was, probably, not trusted by the King—for who could trust him who knew him! —and he had certainly a powerful opponent in his brother Richard, Duke of Gloucester, who, being avaricious and ambitious, wanted to marry that widowed daughter of the Earl of Warwick's who had been espoused to the deceased young Prince, at Calais. Clarence, who wanted all the family wealth for himself, secreted this lady, whom Richard found disguised as a servant in the City of London, and whom he married;

arbitrators appointed by the King, then divided the property between the brothers. This led to ill-will and mistrust between them. Clarence's wife dying, and he wishing to make another marriage which was obnoxious to the King, his ruin was hurried by that means, too. At first, the Court struck at his retainers and dependents, and accused some of them of magic and witchcraft, and similar nonsense. Successful against this small game, it then mounted to the Duke himself, who was impeached by his brother the King, in person, on a variety of such charges. He was found guilty, and sentenced to be publicly executed. He never was publicly executed, but he met his death somehow, in the Tower, and, no doubt, through some agency of the King or his brother Gloucester, or both. It was supposed at the time that he was told to choose the manner of his death, and that he chose to be drowned in a butt of Malmsey wine. I hope the story may be true, for it would have been a becoming death for such a miserable creature.

The King survived him some five years. He died in the forty-second year of his life, and the twenty-third of his reign. He had a very good capacity and some good points, but he was selfish, careless, sensual, and cruel. He was a favourite with the people for his showy manners; and the people were a good example to him in the constancy of their attachment. He was penitent on his death-bed for his "benevolences," and other extortions, and ordered restitution to be made to the people who had suffered from them. He also called about his bed the enriched members of the Woodville family, and the proud lords whose honours were of older date, and endeavoured to reconcile them, for the sake of the peaceful succession of his son and the tranquillity of England.

CHAPTER XXIV.

ENGLAND UNDER EDWARD THE FIFTH.

THE late King's eldest son, the Prince of Wales, called EDWARD after him, was only thirteen years of age at his father's death. He was at Ludlow Castle with his uncle, the Earl of Rivers. The prince's brother, the Duke of York, only eleven years of age, was in London with his mother. The boldest, most crafty; and most dreaded nobleman in England at that time was their uncle RICHARD, Duke of Gloucester, and everybody wondered how the two poor boys would fare with such an uncle for a friend or a foe.

The Queen, their mother, being exceedingly uneasy about this, was anxious that instructions should be sent to Lord Rivers to raise an army to escort the young King safely to London. But, Lord Hastings, who was of the Court party opposed to the Woodvilles, and who disliked the thought of giving them that power, argued

against the proposal, and obliged the Queen to be
satisfied with an escort of two thousand horse.   The
Duke of Gloucester did nothing, at first, to justify sus-
picion.   He came from Scotland (where he was commanding an army) to York, and was there the first to
swear allegiance to his nephew.   He then wrote a
condoling letter to the Queen-Mother, and set off to be
present at the coronation in London.

Now, the young King, journeying towards London
too, with Lord Rivers and Lord Gray, came to Stony
Stratford, as his uncle came to Northampton, about
ten miles distant; and when those two lords heard that
the Duke of Gloucester was so near, they proposed to
the young King that they should go back and greet
him in his name.   The boy being very willing that
they should do so, they rode off and were received with
great friendliness, and asked by the Duke of Gloucester
to stay and dine with him.   In the evening, while they
were merry together, up came the Duke of Buckingham
with three hundred horsemen ; and next morning the
two lords and the two dukes, and the three hundred
horsemen, rode away together to rejoin the King.   Just
as they were entering Stony Stratford, the Duke of
Gloucester, checking his horse, turned suddenly on the
two lords, charged them with alienating from him the

affections of his sweet nephew, and caused them to be
arrested by the three hundred horsemen and taken
back.   Then, he and the Duke of Buckingham went
straight to the King (whom they had now in their
power), to whom they made a show of kneeling down,
and offering great love and submission ; and then they
ordered his attendants to disperse and took him, alone
with them, to Northampton.

A few days afterwards they conducted him to London,
and lodged him in the Bishop's Palace.   But, he did
not remain there long ; for, the Duke of Buckingham
with a tender face made a speech expressing how
anxious he was for the Royal boy's safety, and how
much safer he would be in the Tower until his coronation, than he could be anywhere else.   So, to the
Tower he was taken, very carefully, and the Duke of
Gloucester was named Protector of the State.

Although Gloucester had proceeded thus far with a
very smooth countenance—and although he was a clever
man, fair of speech, and not ill-looking, in spite of one
of his shoulders being something higher than the other
—and although he had come into the City riding bare-
headed at the King's side, and looking very fond of
him—he had made the King's mother more uneasy
yet ; and when the Royal boy was taken to the Tower,

she became so alarmed that she took sanctuary in Westminster with her five daughters.

Nor did she do this without reason, for, the Duke of Gloucester, finding that the lords who were opposed to the Woodville family were faithful to the young King nevertheless, quickly resolved to strike a blow for himself. Accordingly, while those lords met in council at the Tower, he and those who were in his interest met in separate council at his own residence, Crosby Palace, in Bishopsgate Street. Being at last quite prepared, he one day appeared unexpectedly at the council in the Tower, and appeared to be very jocular and merry. He was particularly gay with the Bishop of Ely: praising the strawberries that grew in his garden on Holborn Hill, and asking him to have some gathered that he might eat them at dinner. The Bishop, quite proud of the honor, sent one of his men to fetch some; and the Duke, still very jocular and gay, went out; and the council all said what a very agreeable duke he was! In a little time, however, he came back quite altered— not at all jocular—frowning and fierce—and suddenly said,

"What do those persons deserve who have compassed my destruction; I being the King's lawful, as well as natural, protector?"

To this strange question, Lord Hastings replied, that they deserved death, whosoever they were.

"Then," said the Duke, "I tell you that they are that sorceress my brother's wife;" meaning the Queen; "and that other sorceress, Jane Shore. Who, by witchcraft, have withered my body, and caused my arm to shrink as I now shew you."

He then pulled up his sleeve and shewed them his arm, which was shrunken, it is true, but which had been so, as they all very well knew, from the hour of his birth.

Jane Shore, being then the lover of Lord Hastings, as she had formerly been of the late King, that lord knew that he himself was attacked. So, he said, in some confusion, "Certainly, my Lord, if they have done this, they be worthy of punishment."

"If?" said the Duke of Gloucester; "do you talk to me of ifs? I tell you that they *have* so done, and I will make it good upon thy body, thou traitor!"

With that, he struck the table a great blow with his fist. This was a signal to some of his people outside, to cry "Treason!" They immediately did so, and there was a rush into the chamber of so many armed men that it was filled in a moment.

"First," said the Duke of Gloucester to Lord

Hastings, "I arrest thee, traitor! And let him," he added to the armed men who took him, "have a priest at once, for by St. Paul I will not dine until I have seen his head off!"

Lord Hastings was hurried to the green by the Tower chapel, and there beheaded on a log of wood that happened to be lying on the ground. Then, the Duke dined with a good appetite, and after dinner summoning the principal citizens to attend him, told them that Lord Hastings and the rest had designed to murder both himself and the Duke of Buckingham, who stood by his side, if he had not providentially discovered their design. He requested them to be so obliging as to inform their fellow-citizens of the truth of what he said, and issued a proclamation (prepared and neatly copied out beforehand) to the same effect.

On the same day that the Duke did these things in the Tower, Sir Richard Ratcliffe, the boldest and most undaunted of his men, went down to Pontefract; arrested Lord Rivers, Lord Gray, and two other gentlemen; and publicly executed them on the scaffold, without any trial, for having intended the Duke's death. Three days afterwards the Duke, not to lose time, went down the river to Westminster in his barge, attended by divers bishops, lords and soldiers, and

demanded that the Queen should deliver her second
son, the Duke of York, into his safe keeping. The
Queen, being obliged to comply, resigned the child
after she had wept over him ; and Richard of Gloucester
placed him with his brother in the Tower. Then,
he seized Jane Shore, and, because she had been
the lover of the late King, confiscated her property, and
got her sentenced to do public penance in the streets
by walking in a scanty dress, with bare feet, and
carrying a lighted candle, to St. Paul's Cathedral
through the most crowded part of the City.

Having now all things ready for his own advance-
ment, he caused a friar to preach a sermon at the
cross which stood in front of St. Paul's Cathedral,
in which he dwelt upon the profligate manners
of the late King, and upon the late shame of Jane
Shore, and hinted that the princes were not his
children. " Whereas, good people," said the friar,
whose name was SHAW, " my Lord the Protector, the
noble Duke of Gloucester, that sweet prince, the
pattern of all the noblest virtues, is the perfect image
and express likeness of his father." There had been a
little plot between the Duke and the friar, that the
Duke should appear in the crowd at this moment,
when it was expected that the people would cry " Long

live King Richard!" But, either through the friar
saying the words too soon, or through the Duke's
coming too late, the Duke and the words did not come
together, and the people only laughed, and the friar
sneaked off ashamed.

The Duke of Buckingham was a better hand at such
business than the friar, so he went to the Guildhall
next day, and addressed the citizens in the Lord Protector's behalf. A few dirty men, who had been hired
and stationed there for the purpose, crying when he
had done, " God save King Richard!" he made them a
grave bow, and thanked them with all his heart. Next
day, to make an end of it, he went with the mayor and
some lords and citizens to Baynard Castle, by the river,
where Richard then was, and read an address, humbly
entreating him to accept the Crown of England.
Richard, who looked down upon them out of a window
and pretended to be in great uneasiness and alarm,
assured them there was nothing he desired less, and
that his deep affection for his nephews forbade him to
think of it. To this the Duke of Buckingham replied,
with pretended warmth, that the free people of England
would never submit to his nephew's rule, and that if
Richard, who was the lawful heir, refused the Crown,
why then they must find some else to wear it. The

Duke of Gloucester returned that since he used that strong language, it became his painful duty to think no more of himself and to accept the Crown.

Upon that, the people cheered and dispersed ; and the Duke of Gloucester and the Duke of Buckingham passed a pleasant evening, talking over the play they had just acted with so much success, and every word of which they had prepared together.

CHAPTER XXV.

ENGLAND UNDER RICHARD THE THIRD.

KING Richard the Third was up betimes in the morning, and went to Westminster Hall. In the Hall was a marble seat, upon which he sat himself down between two great noblemen, and told the people that he began the new reign in that place, because the first duty of a sovereign was to administer the laws equally to all, and to maintain justice. He then mounted his horse and rode back to the City, where he was received by the clergy and the crowd as if he really had a right to the throne, and really were a just man. The clergy and the crowd must have been rather ashamed of themselves in secret, I think, for being such poor-spirited knaves.

The new King and his Queen were soon crowned with a great deal of show and noise, which the people liked very much; and then the King set forth on a

royal progress through his dominions.   He was
crowned a second time at York, in order that the
people might have show and noise enough; and
wherever he went was received with shouts of rejoicing
—from a good many people of strong lungs, who were
paid to strain their throats in crying "God save King
Richard!"   The plan was so successful that I am told
it has been imitated since, by other usurpers, in other
progresses through other dominions.

While he was on this journey, King Richard stayed
a week at Warwick.   And from Warwick he sent
instructions home for one of the wickedest murders
that ever was done—the murder of the two young
princes, his nephews, who were shut up in the Tower
of London.

Sir Robert Brackenbury was at that time Governor
of the Tower.   To him, by the hands of a messenger
named JOHN GREEN, did King Richard send a letter,
ordering him by some means to put the two young
princes to death.   But Sir Robert—I hope because he
had children of his own, and loved them—sent John
Green back again, riding and spurring along the dusty
roads, with the answer that he could not do so
horrible a piece of work.   The King having frown-
ingly considered a little, called to him SIR JAMES

TYRREL, his Master of the horse, and to him gave authority to take command of the Tower, whenever he would, for twenty-four hours, and to keep all the keys of the Tower during that space of time. Tyrrel, well knowing what was wanted, looked about him for two hardened ruffians, and chose JOHN DIGHTON, one of his own grooms, and MILES FOREST, who was a murderer by trade. Having secured these two assistants, he went, upon a day in August, to the Tower, showed his authority from the King, took the command for four-and-twenty hours, and obtained possession of the keys. And when the black night came, he went creeping, creeping, like a guilty villain as he was, up the dark stone winding stairs, and along the dark stone passages, until he came to the door of the room where the two young princes, having said their prayers, lay fast asleep, clasped in each other's arms. And while he watched and listened at the door, he sent in those evil demons, John Dighton and Miles Forest, who smothered the two princes with the bed and pillows, and carried their bodies down the stairs, and buried them under a great heap of stones at the staircase foot. And when the day came, he gave up the command of the Tower, and restored the keys, and hurried away without once looking behind him; and

Sir Robert Brackenbury went with fear and sadness to the princes' room, and found the princes gone for ever.

You know, through all this history, how true it is that traitors are never true, and you will not be surprised to learn that the Duke of Buckingham soon turned against King Richard, and joined a great conspiracy that was formed to dethrone him, and to place the crown upon its rightful owner's head. Richard had meant to keep the murder secret; but when he heard through his spies that this conspiracy existed, and that many lords and gentlemen drank in secret to the healths of the two young princes in the Tower, he made it known that they were dead. The conspirators, though thwarted for a moment, soon resolved to set up for the crown against the murderous Richard, HENRY Earl of Richmond, grandson of Catherine : that widow of Henry the Fifth, who married Owen Tudor. And as Henry was of the house of Lancaster, they proposed that he should marry the Princess Elizabeth, the eldest daughter of the late King, now the heiress of the house of York, and thus by uniting the rival families put an end to the fatal wars of the red and white Roses. All being settled, a time was appointed for Henry to come over from

Brittany, and for a great rising against Richard to take place in several parts of England at the same hour. On a certain day, therefore, in October the revolt took place ; but, unsuccessfully. Richard was prepared, Henry was driven back at sea by a storm, his followers in England were dispersed, and the Duke of Buckingham was taken and at once beheaded in the marketplace at Salisbury.

The time of his success was a good time, Richard thought, for summoning a Parliament and getting some money. So, a Parliament was called, and it flattered and fawned upon him as much as he could possibly desire, and declared him to be the rightful King of England, and his only son Edward, then eleven years of age, the next heir to the throne.

Richard knew full well that, let the Parliament say what it would, the Princess Elizabeth was remembered by people as the heiress of the House of York ; and having accurate information besides, of its being designed by the conspirators to marry her to Henry of Richmond, he felt that it would much strengthen him and weaken them, to be beforehand with them, and marry her to his son. With this view he went to the Sanctuary at Westminster, where the late King's widow and her daughter still were, and besought them to come to Court: where (he swore by anything and everything) they should be safely and honorably entertained. They came, accordingly, but had scarcely been at Court a month when his son died suddenly—or was poisoned—and his plan was crushed to pieces.

In this extremity King Richard, always active, thought "I must make another plan." And he made the plan of marrying the Princess Elizabeth himself, although she was his niece. There was one difficulty in the way : his wife, the Queen Anne, was alive. But, he knew (remembering his nephews) how to remove that obstacle, and he made love to the Princess Elizabeth, telling her he felt perfectly confident that the Queen would die in February. The Princess was not a very scrupulous young lady, for, instead of rejecting the murderer of her brothers with scorn and hatred, she openly declared that she loved him dearly; and, when February came and the Queen did not die, she expressed her impatient opinion that she was too long about it. However, King Richard was not so far out in his prediction, but that she died in March—he took good care of that—and then this precious pair hoped to be married. But they were disappointed, for the idea of such a marriage was so unpopular in the country, that the King's chief counsellers,

RATCLIFFE and CATESBY, would by no means under-
take to propose it, and the King was even obliged to
declare in public that he had never thought of such a
thing.

He was, by this time, dreaded and hated by all
classes of his subjects. His nobles deserted every day
to Henry's side; he dared not call another Parliament,
lest his crimes should be denounced there; and, for
want of money, he was obliged to get Benevolences
from the citizens, which exasperated them all against
him. It was said too, that, being stricken by his conscience, he dreamed frightful dreams, and started up in
the night-time, wild with terror and remorse. Active to
the last, through all this, he issued vigorous proclama-
tions against Henry of Richmond and all his followers,
when he heard that they were coming against him with
a Fleet from France; and took the field as fierce and
savage as a wild boar—the animal represented on his
shield.

Henry of Richmond landed with six thousand men
at Milford Haven, and came on against King Richard,
then encamped at Leicester with an army twice as
great, through North Wales. On Bosworth Field, the
two armies met; and Richard, looking along Henry's
ranks, and seeing them crowded with the English

nobles who had abandoned him, turned pale when he
beheld the powerful Lord Stanley and his son (whom
he had tried hard to retain) among them. But, he was
as brave as he was wicked, and plunged into the
thickest of the fight. He was riding hither and
thither, laying about him in all directions, when he
observed the Earl of Northumberland—one of his few
great allies—to stand inactive, and the main body of
his troops to hesitate. At the same moment, his
desperate glance caught Henry of Richmond among a
little group of his knights. Riding hard at him, and
crying " Treason ! " he killed his standard-bearer,
fiercely unhorsed another gentleman, and aimed a
powerful stroke at Henry himself, to cut him down.
But, Sir William Stanley parried it as it fell, and
before Richard could raise his arm again, he was borne
down in a press of numbers, unhorsed, and killed.
Lord Stanley picked up the crown, all bruised and
trampled, and stained with blood, and put it upon
Richmond's head, amid loud and rejoicing cries of
·'Long live King Henry ! "

That night, a horse was led up to the church of the
Grey Friars at Leicester; across whose back was
tied, like some worthless sack, a naked body, brought
there for burial. It was the body of the last of the

Plantagenet line, King Richard the Third, usurper and murderer, slain at the battle of Bosworth Field in the thirty-second year of his age, after a reign of two years.

END OF THE SECOND VOLUME.

BRADBURY AND EVANS, PRINTERS, WHITEFRIARS.

For EU product safety concerns, contact us at Calle de José Abascal, 56–1°,
28003 Madrid, Spain or eugpsr@cambridge.org.

www.ingramcontent.com/pod-product-compliance
Ingram Content Group UK Ltd.
Pitfield, Milton Keynes, MK11 3LW, UK
UKHW040616240426
470322UK00010B/157